THE NEW WAY

21st Century Solutions for America...And the World

Kevin Newsom

ISBN: 9798884674578

Dedicated to the people of the 22nd Century

CONTENTS

Preface

PREFACE

The Current State of Affairs

An Untenable Path

America is at a crossroads. Most people understand that the United States cannot continue on its current path. Yet no one in Washington is capable of charting a new course.

There are great debates, and incredible amounts of grandstanding. But ultimately, both the Democrats and Republicans are unable to repair the damage they have done to our country. So they continue doing the same things over and over again, while hoping for a different result. And the outcome is obvious.

The government of Washington DC is drowning in debt. Wages cannot keep up with the pace of inflation. Prices for food and energy continue to rise. Product shortages and supply chain disruptions, once a rare exception, have now become commonplace. Insurance premiums have reached all-time highs. Exploding housing costs have driven record numbers of people to homelessness. And there's no end in sight.

Politically, Americans have never felt as helpless as they do right now. In response, national leaders continue to employ divide-and-conquer tactics, portraying themselves as defenders of the good and righteous, while demonizing their political opponents as the epitome of evil and wrong. This behavior, combined with the federal government's "one size fits all" approach, has led to levels of alienation and hostility unseen since the Civil War.

The picture overseas is equally as bleak. After two decades of disastrous foreign "adventures", the United States has squandered the favorable reputation it held at the turn of the century. And because of these repeated foreign policy miscalculations, America is now viewed as an aggressive bully, capable of achieving its goals only through coercive force. And as US interventions increase, America's international reputation sinks lower with each passing day.

This situation is untenable. If we keep traveling down this path, the only outcome will be total and utter collapse. Unfortunately, our politicians' only response is to keep doing more of the same. And as a result, they dig us deeper into a hole of deficit spending, war, and endless divide-and-conquer games.

The good news: There are solutions to all these problems. But these solutions require fresh thinking. And a willingness to change. Simply relying on the status quo is no longer an option. If we're going to solve the problems of today, we'll have to find a new way.

--Kevin Newsom
July 7, 2023

1 THE HEART OF THE MATTER

The majority of our government's troubles are due to two factors. First, the distance of government from the people. And second, over-centralization of power.

In the American system, government is a partnership between the people and their representatives. And much like real-world relationships, this partnership depends on close proximity and clear communication. Yet in our current age, what should be a close partnership has turned into a long-distance relationship. The peoples' representatives are in Washington DC far more than they are at home.

This long-distance relationship is further strained by the fact that the people no longer have direct access to their own representatives. Instead, that access is reserved for lobbyists. Specifically, lobbyists from the industries of Finance, Insurance, Real Estate, Defense Contractors, and Pharmaceutical Corporations. Sadly, the average American simply cannot compete with the vast level of resources these industries can offer. And so the people are ignored.

Thus, the distance between government and people is both literal and figurative. Senators and Representatives are physically distant from their constituents for most of the year. At the same time, these representatives are also emotionally and intellectually distant from the people. Citizens who take the time to voice their concerns are lucky to receive a bland form letter as a response. The most fortunate may get to speak to an aide or intern.

This problem of distance is compounded by over-centralization of power. States have been relegated to mere provinces of the federal government. This usurpation of State powers has effectively nullified the voice of the people. And because Washington has accumulated these powers, it views itself as having all the solutions to our problems. Indeed, almost every matter of importance, from social issues and health policies to economics and the environment, is decided at the federal level.

Unfortunately, Washington tends to enrage half of the nation with each "solution" that it offers. And this fact persists regardless of which party controls the federal government. Conservative States and regions don't want to be ruled by progressive leaders. And progressive States and regions don't want to be ruled by conservative leaders.

The problem only gets worse each time a party claims a "mandate" and attempts to impose its will over the entire country. Such attempts to dictate policy typically results in resistance and rebellion among the dissenting States. More importantly, attempts to make "one size fits all" policies alienate the peoples of America from their government...and each other. Simply put: America's size and cultural diversity make over-centralized solutions a recipe for disaster.

Logically, the best solution to these problems is to shorten the distance between the people and their government. And to *decentralize* the powers of the federal government. This book is a blueprint to do just that.

These modifications will go a long way towards solving our most pressing problems. Namely, by returning the bulk of decision-making power to the citizens. And by providing a flexible and responsive government.

It must be stated, however, that even the best-designed Republic still depends upon the citizens to make it work. This means it's up to the people to educate themselves, control themselves, and fully participate in their government. Doing anything less will result in a return to the tenuous spot we currently occupy.

Fortunately, I have the greatest confidence in America. The fires of liberty that began stirring in the 18th century still burn in the hearts and minds of the people. It is up to us to turn that smoldering flame into an inferno...and ensure that America once again lights the way for all those who yearn to be free.

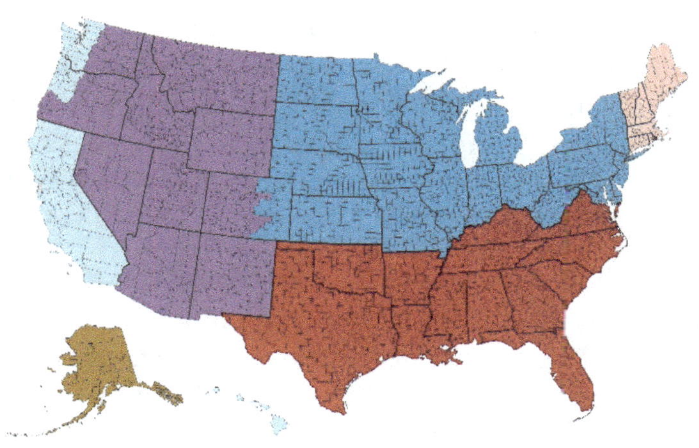

The North American Republic

GDP: $25.6 Trillion

Population: 331,348,115

Square Miles: 3,532,969

This is the North American Republic.[i] The size and scope of the North American government is reminiscent of the general government of America's First Republic. It is a limited government with a few well-defined responsibilities.

The Continental Government's duties are restricted to national defense, the coining of a continental currency, the facilitation of inter-Republic trade, limited taxation, and representing the regional Republics on the international stage. Outside of these specific, enumerated powers, the North American government has very few responsibilities. This is no accident.

Unlike the bloated and chronically-indebted federal government, the Continental Government behaves in a much more restrained and civilized manner. Instead of starting foreign wars, North America will concern itself with foreign trade. In lieu of constant meddling in States' internal affairs, the continental government will encourage each Republic to develop at their own pace. And, instead of being chained to a printing press of soul-crushing debt, the North American government will operate on a balanced budget.

These changes will be quite noticeable to the people of America. Internally, the citizens of the six Republics will enjoy the autonomy to set their own political, social, and economic objectives. And a tremendous variety of lifestyle choices will be available to Americans across the continent. Conservatives, traditionalists, libertarians, liberals, and progressives will all have a home in North America. It's this incredible freedom that will once again be the wonder of the world. And a blessing to mankind.

The following are the six Republics of North America. Each of the Republics operates with a high degree of autonomy. And each Republic can chart their own course on domestic, social, and economic issues. Maximum care was given to the construction of the six Republics. These considerations are primarily based on three factors: Culture, History, and Economics. With the first two categories being of higher importance than the latter.

It's important to note that these Republics may manifest with a different appearance; some counties may opt to stay within their State, while others may choose to leave and form/join other States. Additionally, some States may choose to join a different Republic.

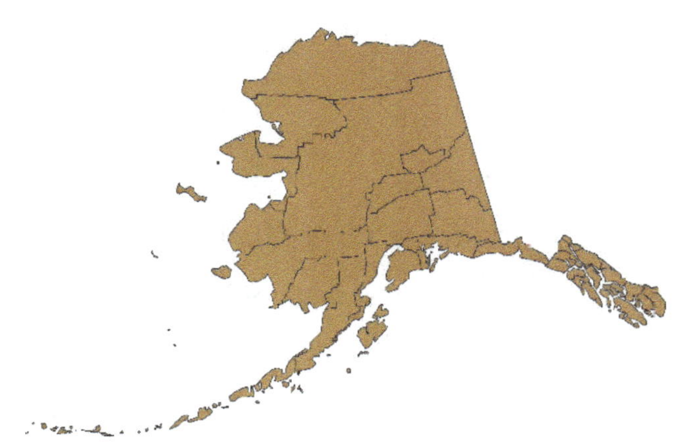

Alaska (Special Status)

GDP: $65.1 Billion

Population: 733,583

Square Miles: 571,022

Nicknamed "The Last Frontier", Alaska represents the northernmost extension of the United States. With over half a million square miles within its borders, it's also the largest geo-graphical State in the US. Interestingly, however, Alaska ranks as the third-lowest populated State in the union.[ii]

The government of Washington DC sends approximately $15 Billion to Alaska annually. Unfortunately, this investment has not encouraged people to move to there. Over the past decade, more people have left Alaska than have immigrated to the State. The sharp decline in working-aged people (aged 20-65) for the past several years is of even greater concern.

Sadly, the DC government seems unable to understand the reality of the situation: People are leaving Alaska because of a lack of opportunities. This includes education, employment, and many of the basic conveniences featured in other States. Under-standing this, it becomes clear that investments need to be centered on creating opportunities that encourage people to im-migrate to the region.

The prioritization of Alaska will focus on the construction and expansion of critical infrastructure. This includes moderniz-ing all major ports to global standards, constructing a first-class bridge across the Bering Strait to facilitate trade, tourism, and mi-gration, and building manufacturing centers for the basic staples of life. The investments will allow the population of the Alaskan

Republic to expand well beyond its current ceiling. All while maintaining the balance of industry and environmentalism that makes the region so special. Instead of being treated as a last frontier, Alaska will become the First Gateway to Eurasia.

This region's main economic drivers include Petroleum, international trade, tourism, logging, mining, and fishing. As the Republic of Alaska's infrastructure improves, it will experience an increase in the service economy, as well as a refocusing on education. The former and the latter will work together to attract young people to move to (and remain in) the Republic.

Geographically, Alaska is the only State to be its own Republic. This is primarily due to its isolation from like-minded States on the continent. There is little shared culture or history with coastal States like Oregon, Washington and California. Additionally, Alaska's need for continual economic support from the national government puts the area in a Special Status among the other Republics. As such, it will maintain a special relationship to the North American government.

Politically, the people of Alaska maintain a strong libertarian streak. This is evidenced by legal marijuana, open carry of firearms without a permit, and few regulations for home schools. This individualistic approach carries over to politics as well; Nearly sixty percent of Alaskan voters identify as belonging to neither party. This strong independent streak will be an asset for the Alaskan Republic. Primarily because it will attract residents (both within and outside of North America) who desire a minimum amount of government interference in their lives. This substantial amount of freedom, combined with a variety of jobs, located in one of the most beautiful places on the planet, make the First Gateway a captivating choice for anyone looking to make a fresh start.

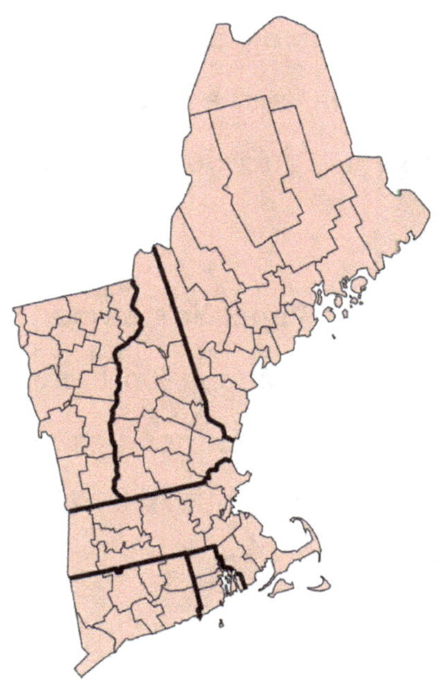

New England

GDP: $1.32 Trillion

Population: 15,129,548

Square Miles: 62,693

New England is the Athens of North America. Each State in the region ranks above the national average for college graduates. Four of the region's States rate in the top ten. All her States reside in the top twenty.

This reliance on education is paying off. As many of New England's textile jobs (a staple of the region's economy) moved south in the mid-twentieth century, several towns in the area transitioned to the technological industry. This was not an overnight process. But it does serve as an excellent example of how a region can leverage its educational base to rebuild its economic engine.

The New England Republic's economy is reliant on manufacturing. This includes weapons (both civilian and defense), industrial and commercial machinery, as well as computers and electronic equipment. Other industries include fishing, tourism, and higher education.

New England's political culture is an interesting mix of progressivism and libertarianism. The region votes heavily democratic in both national and State elections. Democratic candidates have won the region in every Presidential election since 2004. And all six States feature Democratic governors and majorities in their respective Congresses. Curiously, this progressive bent is tempered by States like New Hampshire, which allows open and concealed carry of firearms without a permit, and features no State sales tax *or* State income tax.

New England will enjoy the smoothest transition of all the North American Republics. The political culture is established, the citizens are familiar and comfortable with one another, and, with the possible exception of southwest Connecticut, the geographic boundaries are firmly established. Primary concerns for the region will be the continued evolution of its economy, protecting its natural resources, and attracting young people to move to (and stay in) the New England Republic.

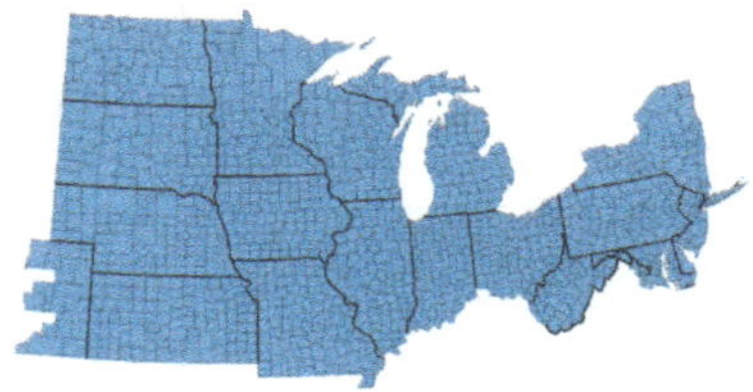

The Northern Republic

GDP: $9.5 Trillion

Population: 123,815,687

Square Miles: 924,417

The Northern Republic represents North America's largest economy. Spanning from the commercial centers of the east to the agricultural heartland of the Midwest and Plains, the Northern States are as dynamic as they are diverse.

Yet a key component of that dynamism, the economic engine, isn't what it used to be. The North is home to the Rust Belt, a region that used to constitute the backbone of global manufacturing. Ranging from New York in the east through Illinois and

Wisconsin in the west, the Rust Belt began losing its manufacturing jobs in the 1970s. This loss of jobs led many to move to other regions of the country. The good news is that, as the US Dollar collapses, manufacturing will come home again. When this happens, the Northern Republic (particularly the Rust Belt States) will be a logical choice for many of these jobs.

Politically, the region features a near-perfect balance of red and blue States. This dichotomy, however, is deceiving. A close inspection of county voting maps reveals that, outside of large metropolitan areas, the majority of the Northern Republic's counties are moderately conservative. So political stability for the Northern States will be best achieved by placing their biggest cities in a semi-autonomous status. This special status will allow large cities to adopt laws that better represent their citizens' desires and preferences...while protecting the desires and wishes of people outside of the cities as well.

Geographically, the Northern Republic has acquired two additional sections: Northeastern Virginia and East Colorado. The five counties of northeast Virginia align more closely with Washington, D.C. than they do with their current State. Likewise, the eighteen counties of East Colorado have much more in common-- politically and culturally-- with their Midwestern neighbors than they do with the Western States.

The primary concerns for the Northern Republic will be the resurrection of manufacturing jobs, providing a special autonomous status for its biggest cities, and making sure its agricultural States are treated fairly. If these objectives are met, the Northern States will enjoy being an economically diverse and culturally attractive region for decades to come.

Pacifica

GDP: $4.76 Trillion

Population: 49,086,355

Square Miles: 202,867

Pacifica is North America's most progressive Republic. Encompassing the States of California, Hawaii, Oregon, and Washington, the politics of the "left coast" are more non-traditional than any other region. This progressive stance is reflected in the region's approach to topics like gun control, gender equality, and abortion.

Of all the regions in North America, Pacifica is the most politically aligned. Each State in the Republic votes overwhelmingly for the Democratic Party. The Pacific Republic is also the most collectivist republic in North America. The region features higher tax rates, as well as the largest social safety net of any location on the continent. In Pacifica, people can actualize into whatever they want. But they'll pay more taxes to do it.

The economy of the region is incredibly diverse. Ranging from technology, manufacturing, media, agriculture, finance and international trade to fishing, logging, education, and tourism, there are plenty of opportunities for people to find interesting and gainful employment. The economic strength of Pacifica is as dynamic as it is impressive. Standing on its own, the Pacific Republic would rank third globally in terms of economic strength.

Geographically, the States of California and Hawaii remain intact. Significant portions of eastern Washington (renamed East Washington) and southern/eastern Oregon (renamed Jefferson) have exited their former States. With both East Washington and Jefferson joining the Western Republic, Pacifica loses significant amounts of territory, but becomes much more culturally cohesive as a result.

One of the chief challenges of the Republic will be the government's tendency to become overbearing and intrusive. Pacifica must find a way to balance its collectivist approach with the rights of individuals to dissent and disagree. Additionally, focusing on finding workable solutions to homelessness and lawlessness in its urban areas is a high priority. If these obstacles can be overcome, the Pacific Republic will continue to be an economic powerhouse, attracting people from all over the world for several generations.

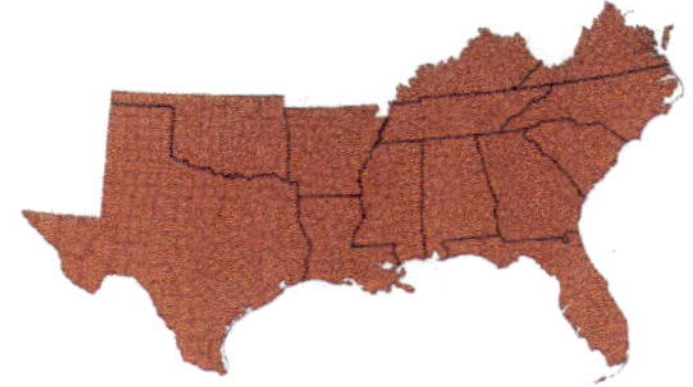

The Southern Republic

GDP: $8.1 trillion

Population: 116,846,018

Square Miles: 831,208

The Southern States are America's most traditional region. Home of the Bible Belt, Christianity maintains a massive influence throughout Southern culture. This is reflected in the South's stances on marriage and abortion, as well as its preference for small government. The ideas of individual liberty and personal responsibility are staples of the Southern Republic's political culture.

The South's form of government closely resembles that of the Articles of Confederation. There exists a loose alliance for purposes of border security and disaster response, as well as interstate trade. Aside from these (and a few other) common issues, each State is practically its own republic.

Economically, the South is diversified, featuring strong connections to petroleum, agriculture, manufacturing, tourism, and international trade. The seaports of Texas, Georgia, South Carolina and Virginia all fall within the top ten ports in the United States. With unfettered access to the markets of Latin America, Eurasia, Africa, and Oceania, the Southern States will prioritize business and trade to increase wealth.

Geographically, the South's current boundaries remain virtually unaltered. There exists one exception: five counties from northeastern Virginia are moved to the Northern States. These counties (Loudoun, Fairfax, Prince William, Stafford, and King George) are heavily influenced by Washington D.C. and have become outliers of most Virginia counties. Aside from this alteration, the Southern States' boundaries remain intact.

The political culture of the South makes for a comfortable and reliable partnership of States. Because of this, the South will be very competitive in the 21st century. Primary concerns include increasing manufacturing and agriculture, investing more revenue into education, and maintaining a diversified economy. If these concerns are addressed, the Southern Republic will enjoy tranquility at home, and abundant trade abroad, for many years to come.

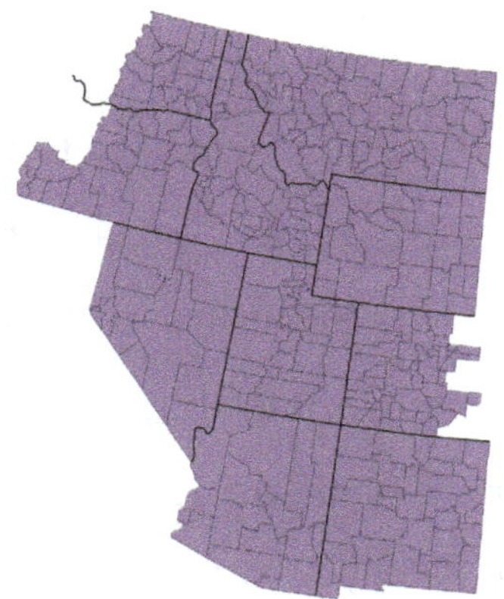

The Western Republic

GDP: $1.77 trillion

Population: 25,736,924

Square Miles: 940,762

The Western States form the largest geographical Republic in North America. Constituting nearly one million square miles, the Western Republic is big and diverse. From the forests of eastern Washington to the deserts of Arizona and New Mexico, the Western States are home to some of the most interesting vistas in North America.

Additionally, three of the five most individualistic States in the nation reside in the West. Amazingly, nearly every single State in the West ranks in the top twenty-five. This strong sense of individualism bears a striking resemblance to that of the American settlers of the region.

Curiously, this individualism has translated into tremendous political diversity. From liberal areas like Colorado and libertarian enclaves such as Montana, to conservative States like Utah, citizens of the Western Republic are sure to find a style of government that suits their needs. And it's the acknowledgment of this variety that will be key to the West's success.

The economy of the Western Republic is extremely multi-faceted. Agriculture, energy, finance, mining, tourism, and forestry are all major industries of the region. As such, the Western government's primary focus will be on natural resource cooperation. With water being the most important of all resources.

The southern half of the Western States rely heavily on the Colorado River for much of their daily water supply. This river begins in the State of Colorado and makes its way to Utah, the Arizona/Nevada border, and then to the California border before flowing to Mexico. This shared resource, along with many other lakes and tributaries, must be effectively managed by the West. Additionally, new means of supplying water to the region, whether that be from desalination or other modalities, will be vital to its prosperity.

Geographically, the Western Republic has acquired East Washington as well as southern/eastern Oregon (renamed the State of Jefferson). Both States are a cultural and political match for the West. The acquisition of East Washington and Jefferson also provides the West with access to the Pacific Ocean. Conversely, the region loses the eighteen counties of East Colorado to the Northern States.

The primary concerns for the West are maintaining a laissez-faire approach to State politics, while simultaneously co-ordinating regional efforts to manage resources. If the Western government achieves this, the Western Republic will thrive as a place of immense political and cultural diversity, as well as abundant natural resources.

3 FOUNDATIONS

The States

The North American Republic is based on two key principles: First, legitimate government operates by the consent of the governed. Second, government functions best when it's close to home.

This is why the States are the foundation of North America. Because it's at the State level the bulk of concerns of the people are addressed. And, most importantly, it's in the States that the people have the greatest impact on their government.

As we transition to this new system, each of the States will retain its current governing structure. Legislatures, courts, and executive systems will all remain intact. Basic functions such as education, criminal justice, and voting will all remain under the purview of State control. This is vital for reasons of consistency, but also to ensure that liberty always resides closest to the people.

Having States as the foundation of government allows for an incredible diversity of political thought. Each State possesses its own unique culture, history and approach to governance. As a result, each State has the potential to spur innovative solutions to the problems of the 21st century. It's been said that in America, States are the laboratories of democracy. In the North American Republic, the States will have the opportunity to live up to that ideal.

The Republics

After the States, the Regional Republics are the next level of governance. They represent the most noticeable --and vital-- change from our current system. This is because the six Republics provide the missing ingredient in American politics: flexibility.

Namely, flexibility for the people to determine their own social and economic policies.

Our current federal system, with its "one size fits all" approach, prohibits the people from determining many of their own laws. Instead, DC attempts to impose its own set of laws on the entire nation. After several decades of this philosophy, the entire federal system has become rigid and incompetent.

This rigidity manifests itself most visibly during Presidential elections. Every four years, candidates promise to "remake America" into their own conservative or progressive utopia. And, as the election comes to an end, the losing party promises to block any and all policies of the new administration. As a result, even the most basic responsibilities of the federal government (such as passing a budget) fail to be accomplished.

The Republics will remedy this problem. Namely, by refocusing the political energies of the people to avenues where their voices are heard. The six Republics will accomplish this by taking on many of the day-to-day functions of the current federal government. This includes regulating interstate commerce of member States, creating/managing disaster response mechanisms, and coordinating common approaches to social issues like abortion and gun control.

This serves a dual purpose. First, it brings the vast majority of everyday governance back to the people. Second, the shifting of many basic responsibilities to the Republics will free the North American government to focus on its Constitutionally-defined duties.

It's important to note that no two Republics will be exactly alike. While each Republic will feature similar structures, the scope of their governments will be determined by the people of their member States. For example, some regions, such as the South, will feature a minimalist approach, where each State is practically its own Republic. Other regions, like Pacifica, will likely determine that a close-knit, collectivist strategy is better suited to their needs.

These differences among regional Republics provide the flexibility that's missing from the current federal system. And it's this flexibility that allows the people of each region to create governments that more accurately represent them. This flexibility will allow each of the Republics to tackle the day-to-day business of governance with less partisan warfare...and a greater sense of purpose.

This regional system minimizes hyper-partisanship by combining States of similar culture, history, and economics together. This brings the bulk of day-to-day governance back to the people. Because each Republic is guided and managed by its member States. And each State is guided and managed by the people.

The Continental Government

The Continental government is the third and final layer of governance for the peoples of America. It serves as the "national" government of the North American Republic. The appearance of the Continental government closely resembles that of the current federal government. It still features an elected President and Congress, and institutions like the Supreme Court, Electoral College, and Department of Defense. And its location is still in Washington, DC.

Substantial differences rest in the size and scope of the two systems. Unlike the federal system, the Continental government's powers will be limited to the most basic Constitutional functions. These functions include:Continental defense, the coining and creation of sound money, regulating inter-Republic trade and disputes, creating and maintaining a balanced budget, and representing the Republics on the international stage.

These limitations are for the benefit of the people of North America. Because the bulk of social and economic issues will be decided at the State/Regional level, national elections will become far less contentious. Gone will be the endless debates over social issues. Because those issues will be decided at the State level. Gone will be the constant battles to "remake America". Because it will be the *people* who decide how America is made, via their State and Regional elections.

This will spare Americans much of the chaos, grief, and violence that has now become commonplace during the quadrennial election cycle. And allow for a much more efficient and effective administration of the national government.

Presidential elections under the North American Republic will be relatively routine and business-like. The same can be said for day-to-day life in the Continental government. Because the most controversial social issues will be decided at the State/Regional level, the legislature (and executive branch) can focus their time on matters pertaining to national-level government. This will undoubtedly change the composition of those who run for Congress and the Presidency. Instead of the embarrassing, virtue-signaling sideshow we've become accustomed to, national candidates will be expected to focus on issues assigned to the Continental government. So, we can expect (and demand) a much higher quality of representative than we've endured in recent years.

The Continental government's assigned powers are noticeably less in number than the sprawling bureaucracy of the federal system. This should not be interpreted as a statement that this new government is somehow unimportant or unnecessary. On the contrary, the responsibilities of the Continental government are immense. And its success will greatly depend on the wisdom and skill of those elected to its offices.

4 STRUCTURES

The States

Of all the layers of North American government, the States will see the least amount of change. Governors and legislatures will still be elected in the same manner as before. Each State will still determine their own approach to voting, criminal justice, and budget issues. Local governments will retain the structures they currently enjoy. And most States will maintain the exact same political dynamics that they currently feature.

There are two reasons for this. First, State government works. State and local governments generally represent the needs and desires of their people. And if they don't, their people are close enough to the levers of power that they can organize and remove representatives that are harmful or negligent in their duties.

Second, keeping our State structures intact makes for an easier transition to the new system. Most Americans still trust their State and local governments. So maintaining our State governments as they currently exist will help assure as smooth a transition to the new system as possible.

Exceptions to this include States that gain or lose counties. Clearly, in such a case, adjustments will have to be made to account for changes in a State's territory. These adjustments will include both function (changes to tax base) and changes in structure (such as the composition of legislatures).

The most notable changes will occur for those living in new States like Jefferson and East Washington. The creation of capital cities, legislatures, and election cycles will take some time. The good news is that each new State will be able to utilize already-existing election precincts and congressional districts to build their political infrastructure. And States that need financial assistance will be able to rely upon their regional partners, as well as the Continental government, for help.

For most Americans, life inside their States will be exactly the same as it was before the transition. This is no accident. Many Americans still trust and rely upon their States. And State and local governments still offer the best representation for their people. So it's vital to ensure State structures remain virtually untouched as we transition to the new system.

The Republics

The Republics represent the most visible change in the new system. This is because five of the six regional Republics will be entirely new structures. And they'll be built from the ground up. By the people.

Each Republic (apart from Alaska) will feature an elected regional legislature and President. Each region will also have its own capital city, which will house their legislature and President. The terms of office, as well as election procedures, will be determined by the people of their member States. The structures (and functions) of every Republic will be codified into a regional Constitution. This Constitution will be ratified by each member State, via State Convention. It will clearly delineate the roles of each regional government, and the mechanisms involved with its successful operation.

The structures/functions of each Republic will vary depending upon the will of the people. Some Republics will feature a very minimalist approach, where their member States retain the bulk of decision-making authority. Other regions will prefer a more centralized/collectivist approach. While yet others will prefer a hybridized arrangement, in which States hold the bulk of powers for some issues but cede power to their regional Republics for other matters. This kind of flexibility is key for the new system. Primarily because it ends the disastrous "one size fits all" approach. Additionally, this openness to new ideas and techniques will focus the creativity of the American peoples towards innovative solutions for our most pressing problems.

While the structural *differences* among Republics will be a blessing, there are also important *similarities* to make note of. First, each Republic is required to adopt the US Constitution as the supreme law of the land. This includes all the individual freedoms enumerated in the Bill of Rights, as well as Amendments concerning equal protection under the law. This is non-negotiable and a requirement for any Republic to join North America.

Second, each Republic is required to operate with a balanced budget. A broke regional government would naturally reach out to the national government for a bailout. And, as we've seen so often in the federal system, that bailout would come with strings attached. These strings would eventually lead to total control of the Republics by the national government. And this would defeat the purpose of having the Republics in the first place. As such, it's important for the Republics to operate within their means.

Third, none of the regional Republics may enter a defense/trade alliance with any country outside of the North American Republic. This is common sense. Any such alliance would inevitably lead to military entanglements, internecine war, and the destruction of peace and prosperity across the continent. Aside from these commonalities, the Republics have a free hand to decide their own internal policies and structures.

The Continental Government

The appearance of the Continental government is almost identical to the current federal system. In the new system, there exist the familiar three branches of government; the legislative, executive and judicial. Members of the three branches are elected/ appointed in the same fashion as they are in the federal system. And the length of each term of office remains the same; Presidents serve four-year terms, Representatives two-year terms, and Senators six-year terms.

The differences between the Continental and federal systems are less focused on appearance, and more focused on structure. In other words, the two systems will look very similar. The key difference resides in how the two governments *function.*

First and foremost, the United States Constitution is the Supreme Law across the North American Republic. All the individual freedoms enshrined in the document will remain intact. Only slight adjustments will be made to account for the emergence of the regional Republics, as well as a more precise delineation of the functions of the Continental Government. Expressed powers of the Continental Government include Taxation, Paying Debts & Borrowing Money, Maintaining Continental Defense, Regulating Inter-Republic Trade and Disputes, Coining Money, Establishing Post Offices, Protecting Patents & Copyrights, Establishing Lower Courts, and Declaring War. These duties will constitute the bulk of the Continental Government's responsibilities.

Each branch of the current federal system will be affected by these changes. Fortunately, these modifications will bring increases in efficiency and effectiveness to each respective branch. And, more importantly, safeguard the liberty and tranquility of Americans by placing clear limits on how the Continental Government operates.

The Legislative Branch

Of all three branches of the federal government, Congress has consistently garnered the lowest approval ratings. Generally, the American people score their federal legislature at an approval rate of less than ten percent. So the legislative branch will receive the lion's share of improvements in the new system.

One of the glaring problems of the federal system is the existence of the "career politician". As the federal government has continued to metastasize into all areas of public/private life, the opportunities for graft and corruption have become overwhelming. So much so that the office of Representative or Senator is now highly coveted for its potential job security. It's not uncommon for people to ride out twenty, thirty, or even forty years in Congress. All while accumulating vast amounts of personal wealth and influence.

This behavior leads to the establishment of fiefdoms throughout the halls of Washington. Representatives and Senators get enormously wealthy trading stocks, investing in corporations, and entering the revolving door of regulation/employment at various industries. All at the expense of the American taxpayer.

The Continental system fixes this problem by introducing term limits on members of Congress. Under the new system, Representatives are limited to a total of three terms, and Senators to a total of two terms. These limits apply to each person over the course of their lifetimes. So, regardless of whether a person serves individual or consecutive terms, they are still limited to a total of three terms in the House and two in the Senate for as long as they live.

The implementation of term limits will have the twin benefit of keeping "legacy" style corruption to a minimum. While also allowing for a greater diversity of Representatives and Senators into Congress. Legislatures are akin to the nation's circulatory system. To stay healthy, we must keep a steady flow of blood through the body. The establishment of term limits ensures that the process continues unabated. And goes a long way to removing the clogs in America's arteries.

Due to the establishment of the regional Republics, our Representatives and Senators will find that their time and energy will be much more narrowly focused. Because the bulk of social issues will be determined at the State and regional level, members of Congress will be able to focus on issues of true importance.

One such issue of importance is the budget. The Continental Congress will be required to pass a balanced budget every year. Completion of the budget won't be an option. It will be required to be the first bill introduced at the beginning of each legislative session, and it must be finalized before the end of the session. In other words, crafting a budget will be a top priority of the legislature. Because in the North American Republic, annual deficits (and the resulting bottomless pit of debt) will be a thing of the past.

The Annual Balanced Budget (ABB) will be a bedrock of the Continental Government. No riders (or other unrelated extras) may be attached to the document. This will ensure that the only items listed in the budget are the budget itself. And the bill that's passed will be prominently published, both in print and online, so that the people of America can see exactly where their money is going.

Other structural changes include a law prohibiting legislators from purchasing publicly-traded stock while in office. The temptation to utilize inside information to enrich themselves has proven too great to withstand. Therefore, members of the Continental Congress are prohibited from buying any public stocks while in office. Senators and Representatives are free to keep or sell what they have during their term. But the days of leveraging insider knowledge for private enrichment will be over.

One vital arena for change is the issue of dual citizenship. The federal government allows Americans to acquire dual citizenship with over 60 countries. While splitting time between two countries is wonderful for private citizens, the issue becomes problematic inside the legislature. Currently, there are no restrictions placed on members of Congress maintaining dual citizenship with foreign nations. This represents an incredible conflict of interest.

An elected member of Congress is expected to make decisions that benefit their constituents (and the United States) first and foremost. Yet if a member of Congress is a citizen of two different countries, how can we be assured that they will always make decisions for *America,* and not their "other" homeland? How can we be assured that decisions will not be made due to a sense of loyalty to a legislator's "alternate" home country? Indeed, for issues such as security, intelligence, and defense, having divided loyalties can (and will) yield disastrous results.

When it comes to foreign relations in the 21st century, the stakes are too high for divided loyalties. That's why one of the requirements to serve in Congress is the renunciation of any citizenship from outside of the North American Republic. By ending the practice of dual-citizen representatives, we remove one more opportunity for graft and corruption, and ensure that Congress' focus remains on America, first and foremost.

The structural changes placed on the Continental Congress will produce a more efficient and representative legislature As always, it will be up to the people to keep a tight leash on their Senators and Representatives. The price of freedom is eternal vigilance. And the North American system will help the people to maintain said vigilance for many years to come.

The Executive Branch

Of the three branches of government, the Executive Branch routinely garners the most attention. And for good reason. A modern American President has more power than any leader in human history. As the Commander-In-Chief of the Armed Forces, Presidents can direct military interventions into almost every corner of the globe. Even more importantly, US Presidents have the sole authority to launch nuclear strikes into foreign countries. These two abilities alone provide the President with unimaginable power. Yet it's the other, less noticeable powers that affect Americans more directly.

Most notably: The Executive Branch features fifteen departments that interact with the American people daily. Each of the fifteen departments features a leader appointed by the President (and approved by the US Senate). These department secretaries report directly to the President and steer their respective departments in the direction the President deems most appropriate.

The problem with this arrangement is, due to the bloated nature of the federal government, many of these departments have overgrown their original scope. More alarmingly, a handful have become abusive towards the people. It's for this reason that many departments must be pruned...both financially as well as administratively.

Department of Education

The Department of Education (DoED) was established by Congress in 1980. Its stated purpose is to: "promote student achievement and preparation for global competitiveness by fostering educational excellence and ensuring equal access".[iii]

Domestic departments like Education must be reconfigured to focus on research and advice. The DoED's purpose is not to constantly interject itself into the States. Nor is it to set standards for each school district around the country. The DoED was designed to complement the efforts of the States to educate their children. This will be best accomplished by focusing on researching the best practices of teaching children reading, writing, arithmetic, as well as basic life skills, and then sharing the results of this research with all public schools.

The bulk of financial obligations for the DoED is for Student Aid. This includes direct student loans as well as financial assistance. In 2023, seventy-seven percent of the department's $270 Billion budget (approximately $208 Billion) was allocated to Student Aid.[iv] This financial aid for higher education reaches over ten million students per year.

In the North American Republic, financial aid for students will continue to be a priority. The key differences will reside in how that aid is distributed. While students of all majors/specialties will be eligible for assistance, priority will be placed on majors/tracks that are the most vital for the future of the Republic. For example, fields such as Epidemiology, Nursing, Machine Learning, Energy, and Public Administration represent areas of key importance for the 21st century. Fields such as these will be prioritized when it comes to the distribution of financial aid.

The Department of Education's current expenditures represent about two percent of the federal budget. This is a very reasonable target for the North American Republic, especially when one considers the benefits of higher education to society. Loans will be directly distributed to students from each Republic at an interest rate of 3%. These loans will be repayable for a period of ten years after the student completes their education and will not be collectible unless the borrower is working.

Department of Defense

The United States War Department was founded by Congress in 1789. In 1948 it was renamed the Department of Defense (DOD). The DOD's focus is the military defense of the United States. The Defense Department is one of the most necessary elements of government. The DOD budget for fiscal year 2024 is $886 Billion.[v]

Obviously, this defense budget is quite large. So large, in fact, that the United States spends more on defense annually than

China, Russia, India, the United Kingdom, France, Germany, and Japan combined! With that kind of financial power, one would expect the US military to have the most advanced and reliable equipment in the world. Sadly, that isn't always the case.

Because private corporations (known as defense contractors) manufacture most of the weapons for the US government, there can be significant variations in quality. Every day we hear stories of planes that can't fly, earplugs that don't block sound, and vehicles suffering from dry-rotted tires. Like any corporation, defense contractors are always looking to maximize their profits. And to do that, they often cut corners.

And one of the most visible corners is the sourcing of components for complex weapons systems. When contractors are seeking large quantities of basic items such as transistors, they will look for the lowest price possible. This often leads them to buying components from places like China. The very same China that the United States government deems a strategic competitor. It doesn't take a rocket scientist to see the flaws in this system. Allowing potential adversaries to be the source of materials for one's defense apparatus is thoroughly insane. The possibilities for sabotage and other mischief are too great for any rational person to justify.

To put it simply, the days of outsourcing our defense to other countries must end. Unlike its federal predecessor, the North American DOD will be supported by a Military-Industrial Complex (MIC) that can produce everything it needs inside North America. This will require rebuilding the MIC into a "closed loop" system, in which each step of development, from Research and Design, sourcing of materials, manufacturing, testing, and mass production, occurs within North America itself.

The closed loop system will also require that each segment of the MIC must be a part of the Department of Defense. In other words, private corporations will no longer be able to exploit and overcharge the government for components of our defense supply chain. In the North American Republic, all major aspects of the MIC will be a part of the Defense Department, and accountable to the American people.

In the 20th century, late-night comedians had a field-day joking about the military being charged fifty-thousand dollars for each toilet seat. Sadly, this wasn't an exaggeration. Since private corporations are a key part of defense production in the United States, they can get away with charging the government outrageous prices for the most basic components.

Unfortunately, this problem has only gotten worse in the 21st century. An example being the F-35 Lightning, which will cost American taxpayers a whopping $1.7 trillion to produce. This fleet of planes was designed to "do it all". Unfortunately, significant numbers of the aircraft can't do *anything*. As they are routinely grounded due to faulty engines, or the need for general repairs.[vi]

Because the DOD relies on private corporations to research and build its planes, the Defense Department must wait for these corporations to figure out the problems with their designs before any repairs can take place. This results in large numbers of aircraft being perpetually unavailable to the Armed Forces. These kinds of delays in the supply chain are not only wasteful, but dangerous as well. One can imagine being caught in an emergency, or a prolonged war, and only having half of our planes able to get in the air.

This is an unacceptable situation! And yet, under the federal system, this kind of gross ineptitude not only continues unabated, but is actively rewarded! Private military contractors typically report profits of billions of dollars each year. Regardless of the success or failure of the products they sell.

Nationalizing the top defense contractors will go a long way towards eliminating the corruption in the current MIC. Because all segments of the production process will be managed by the North American government, the focus of the MIC will shift from profits and waste to efficiency and effectiveness. As such, the DOD will be motivated to keep quality high, and expenditures under budget.

The good news is that this nationalization will be seamless in its execution. Primarily because it will require no changes in personnel. And very few, if any, changes in each company's structure. Each worker (from janitor all the way up to CEO) will retain his/her salary, benefits, and job description. The difference will be that, instead of cutting corners to make a fast buck, each defense contractor will work to make the best possible product, using parts sourced from inside North America.

These changes will have the benefit of eliminating the waste and increasing the efficiency of the Defense Department. And this new defense policy will create thousands of American manufacturing jobs. Since all facets of weapons procurement will be completed inside North America, there will be numerous opportunities for employment at every step of the process. And that's a win/win for the American peoples.

Department of Transportation

The Department of Transportation (DOT) was established by Congress in 1966. Its main mission is to deliver federal transportation systems to the American people. These transportation systems take many forms, from roads and highways, to airports, railroads, waterways and even pipelines.

Since its founding, the DOT has steadily expanded its jurisdiction. It's now a massive umbrella organization that includes the Federal Aviation Administration (FAA), the Maritime Administration, and the Pipeline and Hazardous Materials Safety Administration (PHMSA). As of the time of publication, the Transportation Department's requested budget is $108 Billion.[vii] This hefty allotment has allowed the DOT to further grow its services to include offering grants to communities who wish to expand local transportation options, underwriting ferry services for rural areas, and assisting small seaports with infrastructure.

While most of these services are certainly wonderful, problems begin to emerge when one considers the state of the US economy. Currently, the federal government operates with an annual deficit of $1.7 trillion. This kind of deficit spending is completely out of control. And it must be reined in if the country is to have any kind of future.

Understanding this, one can expect the budget for the DOT (and other federal agencies) will soon be reduced dramatically. Therefore, the Department of Transportation must re-prioritize its goals. Special focus will be placed on Continent-wide transportation systems, such as highways, airports, railroads, seaports, and pipelines. After the construction and maintenance of those systems are taken care of, remaining funds must be utilized wisely. The end of deficit spending signals the end of bloated budgets for federal agencies. This means that several of the side projects from the DOT will have to be eliminated. And many of these projects involve assisting State and local governments with transportation issues.

The good news is that in the North American Republic, regional governments will lighten the load for the DOT. Each of the Regions are closer to State and local governments, both geographically and culturally. So they will have a better understanding of what transportation projects are most urgently needed at any given time. And, because of this proximity, the Regions can complete said projects in a more timely and cost-effective manner.

As a result, the Department of Transportation will be able to spend its remaining time and resources on research and development. The techniques and information gathered from this R&D will then be shared with the Regions, States, and local governments. And they will be free to utilize this information as they see fit.

In the NAR, the Department of Transportation will play a vital role in building and maintaining the Continent's transportation infrastructure. It, along with the other federal agencies, will learn to operate within a sensible budget, and adjust its priorities to national projects, as well as Research and Development. This DOT will be efficient, effective, and provide large swaths of useful data to the Regions, States, and local governments across North America.

Department of Health and Human Services

The Department of Health, Education and Welfare was established by Congress in 1953. When Education was spun off as its own entity in 1980, the structure was reorganized as the Department of Health and Human services (HHS). The HHS mission is to enhance the health and well-being of all Americans.

The HHS is an incredibly large bureaucracy; it contains several vital agencies such as the Centers for Disease Control (CDC), the Food and Drug Administration (FDA), and The National Institutes for Health (NIH). Additionally, the HHS oversees the Centers for Medicare and Medicaid Services (CMS), which administers the nation's Medicare program, and partners with the States for administration of Medicaid and The Children's Health Insurance Program (CHIP). These agencies constitute what is arguably the most important Department (along with Defense) in the President's cabinet.

Clearly, the HHS is a department that millions of Americans rely upon every single day. Understanding this, ensuring the department receives full funding will be a top priority of the North American government. For reference: In 2023, the budget for the HHS was $1.7 trillion.[viii] Total funding for the HHS represented approximately 25% of the federal budget in 2023. In the

NAR, this level of commitment to seniors and the less fortunate will continue. A budget range of 25% for the health of the people is an acceptable target.

Perhaps the most important aspect of healthcare is providing accurate information. People who have the best possible information are more likely to make the best possible choices. Unfortunately, some departments of the HHS have done a miserable job of providing accurate and truthful information.

Specifically, the Centers for Disease Control (CDC) failed to adequately inform Americans about the experimental nature of medical products it recommended people to inject into their systems. Millions of Americans were "mandated" to inject vaccines that they had no idea were classified as experimental. And they were shocked to learn that, should they become ill (or die) from these experimental drugs, they could not sue the vaccine manufacturers for medical compensation.

The Food and Drug Administration (FDA) made matters even worse. Upon receiving Freedom of Information (FOIA) requests from doctors to reveal the data used to determine said vaccines were "safe", the FDA stated that they wouldn't provide said data to the public for seventy-five years![ix] The FDA then claimed that they just didn't have the manpower to release the data at a faster rate. The administration attempted to escape responsibility for failing to provide vaccine safety data because there is no law requiring them to do so in an expeditious manner. Fortunately, in the case of the FDA's attempted slow walk, a federal judge ruled that they had to release said data within eight months.

In the North American Republic, this failure and corruption will cease to exist. First, the Continental Congress will pass a law requiring the CDC to produce informed consent pamphlets with every dose of experimental drugs provided to consumers. These pamphlets will explain to the potential user that the drug is experimental, not fully approved for consumption, and that the customer will have no legal recourse for compensation should injury or death occur. This form will be required to be signed by the customer should he or she choose to go forward with ingesting/injecting said drug.

Second, the FDA's "hide-and-seek" antics will come to an end. The Continental Congress will create a law that requires the FDA to publish (both in print and online) all safety data for all approved/experimental drugs no later than 60 days after their approval/emergency use authorization. More importantly, decision-makers in both agencies who were involved in the botched pandemic response will be terminated from employment. And they will be fully prosecuted for any crimes committed.

Additionally, in the NAR, the revolving door of regulating Big Pharma and then going to work for Big Pharma will be permanently closed. Those who wish to make money working for drug manufacturers are free to do so. And those who wish to protect the American peoples will be free to work for the CDC/FDA. But the days of bouncing back and forth between the two will be over.

Staying within the realm of the FDA, improvements in food labeling will be commonplace in the NAR. Specifically, in North America all food products containing Genetically Modified Organisms (GMOs), aka, "Bio Engineered" ingredients, must be labeled as such. Food manufacturers have, for several years, lobbied the US Congress to prevent people from knowing if their products are genetically modified. This disgusting act of hiding ingredients will come to an end. The people have a right to know exactly what is in their food. And this includes whether their groceries contain Bio Engineered products.

Another area of vital importance is the National Emergency Room Crisis. Because quick access to quality care is so limited, millions of people end up going to the emergency room to have their basic medical needs met. So much so that it's not uncommon to encounter hours-long waits just to be triaged. Clearly, this is an unsustainable situation. Emergency rooms were never designed to be "overflow" systems for basic healthcare. They are in place to deal with serious, extreme, or life-or-death medical issues.

The North American government will ease the burden on emergency rooms. Primarily by working with the States and Regions to construct Local Clinics (LCs). These local clinics will serve people who experience medical issues that need immediate attention but fall short of a life-or-death situation. These Local Clinics will be able to handle all minor emergencies for the people in their community. They will be managed by experienced doctors, physician's assistants, and nurses. And staffed by students from medical and nursing schools.

Local Clinics will help alleviate much of the pressure from emergency rooms across the country. By handling the overflow of pressing, but non-life-threatening issues, LCs will free up space in the ERs across the country. This extra space will translate to more time that can be dedicated to those suffering from the most serious of medical conditions. Because in an emergency, every second counts.

When a child develops a high fever in the middle of the night, an elderly person falls and breaks their arm, or an adult develops a stomach pain that won't go away, the Local Clinic system will be available to assist them in the shortest time possible. North America's HHS will help States and Regions construct these Local Clinics throughout the Republic. Because efficient and effective healthcare should be available to every citizen. Whether that's for relatively minor injuries and illnesses, or significant health emergencies.

There is much work to be done in the HHS. Several agencies have been derelict in their duties. These agencies will be disciplined and brought into alignment with the values of the North

American Republic. Once this happens, the people of America will benefit greatly, and enjoy longer, healthier, and more enjoyable lives.

Department of Housing and Urban Development

The Department of Housing and Urban Development (HUD) was created by Congress in 1965. The HUD mission, according to its website, is: "to create strong, sustainable, inclusive communities and quality affordable homes for all."[x] The budget for HUD in 2023 was $61 Billion.[xi]

Curiously, when one looks around the United States, affordable housing is nowhere to be seen. At the time of publication, prices for houses and apartment rents are at all-time highs. At no point in American history has basic housing been so unaffordable as it is right now. It's safe to say that there is a full-blown housing crisis in America.

There are many culprits for this crisis. One of which is corporations buying up single-family homes and then selling them (or renting them out) for huge profits. The companies who do this may take the form of banks, private investment firms, or massive Wall Street corporations. But regardless of the form these companies take, the result is always the same: fewer homes available for purchase and higher prices for the people.

In the North American Republic, Congress will pass a law prohibiting investment firms, banks and corporations from purchasing already-built homes as investments. Additionally, all such entities maintaining reserves of already-built homes will be required to sell said houses, at fair-market value. To prevent market volatility, this sell-off will occur at a rate of 33% of their accumulated, already-built houses per year. This law will also provide tax incentives to corporations and developers to build new homes. These incentives will include tax-free building supplies and the waiving of permits and other regulatory fees (subject to the approval of each respective State).

As this is occurring, it will be HUD's job to monitor the housing market. And to make sure extreme shortages (or excesses) are avoided in the future. As the market stabilizes, and housing for every American becomes affordable, HUD will alert the Congress that the incentives on building can be sunsetted for a time. It's important to note that this law will not prohibit banks from purchasing homes via mortgage agreement, or from foreclosing on homes due to delinquent payments. The purpose of this law is to prevent the predatory investment practices that the American peoples have suffered under for the past decade.

In the North American Republic, HUD will also play a key role in the development of new housing. This includes the utilization of environmentally friendly materials, as well as completely new concepts and designs. Is there a more efficient way to build a single-family home? Is there a way to design apartments to increase privacy and lower cost? Can housing become portable? Recyclable? Research and Design will be a key component of HUD in the NAR. And this research will be shared with all the States and Regions.

Finally, HUD (working alongside the Department of Transportation) will provide a thorough analysis of North America's infrastructure. With recommendations on which urban areas and transportation structures are in good shape, which need repairs, and which are not worth repairing. This data will then be shared with the States and Regions.

In the North American Republic, the Department of Housing and Urban Development will be a key player in the Executive Branch. Since quality and affordable housing is a basic human requirement, HUD will continue to play a vital role in American government throughout the 21st century.

Department of the Treasury

The United States Dollar has been the world's reserve currency for eighty years. This reserve status has been a tremendous boon for Washington. Primarily because it allows the D.C. government to run substantial budget deficits each year. And, consequently, to carry a massive debt (approaching $36 trillion at the time of publication!) with virtually zero fiscal consequences.

This advantageous situation exists for several reasons. Firstly, the dollar's status as world reserve currency was established immediately after World War II. With Germany and Japan in ruins, and the Soviet Union recovering from a loss of over 25 million people, the United States became the planet's manufacturing hub. And for the next several years, the US economy was unquestionably dominant.

For countries around the world, it was a wise decision to hold a large reserve of US dollars. Because not only was the United States the world's largest economy, but it was also the most stable political unit on the planet. So, holding US dollars was a reliable place to store wealth. Eventually, many nations also began using dollars to buy and sell goods from other countries. This reliance on dollars as an international medium of exchange was deepened in 1974.

In that year, the United States and Saudi Arabia made a very important deal.[xii] In exchange for US military protection and political support, the government of Saudi Arabia agreed to only accept US dollars when it sold its oil to foreign countries.

In many ways, the United States accomplished a master stroke in the world of international politics. By pegging its currency to the sale of one of the most vital products on the planet, it guaranteed the nations of the world would carry substantial reserves of US Dollars. Thereby keeping the value of the dollar high. And allowing the United States government to spend what it wanted with little to no repercussions.

To those paying attention, one thing became abundantly clear: the strength of the United States was dependent upon the strength of the dollar. And, despite continued deficit spending by the federal government, this immense strength continued to blossom from the mid-70s through the end of the 1990s. But as time moved on, so did the reality of the world. By the early 21st century, Russia, China, and a host of other nations began making moves to de-dollarize their economies. And by so doing, to lessen US dominance.

This started with countries like China and Brazil agreeing to use their own currencies in bilateral trade. These bilateral trade agreements began to proliferate in the early 2020s. Most notably, in 2022 China and Saudi Arabia inked a deal in which Saudi will sell its oil to China in exchange for China's currency, the Yuan.[xiii] As China is the largest importer of Saudi oil in the world, this deal could have dramatic consequences for US dollar dominance. Particularly if the government of Saudi Arabia agrees to a similar arrangement with other countries. Or, more strikingly, if Saudi mandates that all its oil sales will be conducted with the Yuan.

It's obvious that the dollar's status as world reserve currency is being eroded. As more and more countries abandon the dollar in bilateral trade, and the sale of oil and other goods continues to be de-pegged from the US currency, the amount of dollars held by foreign countries will decrease. Ultimately, this will result in a currency that few (if any) countries feel the need to use. And if other countries don't feel the need to hold large reserves of the dollar, the US will not be able to get away with its "bottomless pit" of deficit spending and debt.

All of which will mean the United States will have to live *within* its means. The consequence of such a scenario is a significant reduction in government spending...and an equally significant reduction of US reach across the globe. As the trend of de-dollarization continues, and the end of the dollar as world reserve currency draws nearer, the Treasury Department should be ready to act. Namely, by ditching the Federal Reserve Note and re-issuing the Greenback. This "new dollar" will be available in both digital and physical currency.

If not completed beforehand, one of the first acts of the North American Congress will be to repeal the Federal Reserve Act and re-establish sound money to the American peoples. This Sound Money Act, in addition to stabilizing the North American economy, will also feature a requirement that physical cash be accepted in all businesses for a period of no less than fifty years. To have a sound country, one must have a sound currency. Creating and maintaining this sound currency will be a top priority of the North American Republic. And job number one for the Treasury Department.

Department of Homeland Security

Formed in 2003, the Department of Homeland Security (DHS) is responsible for the public security of the United States. The DHS is a huge department, trailing only the DOD and Department of Veterans Affairs in the number of employees. Some of the agencies under its jurisdiction include the US Border Patrol, Immigration and Naturalization Service (INS), Transportation and Security Administration (TSA), Federal Emergency Management Agency (FEMA), the Coast Guard, and the Secret Service. It's annual budget at the time of publication is $103 billion.[xiv]

As a cabinet organization, the DHS is ultimately under the control of the President. So the policies of the department can change drastically from one administration to the next. Unfortunately, large bureaucracies are not designed for such wild swings in direction...especially in four-year time spans.

The effects of extreme policy swings are most visible on the US border. Under some administrations, the Border Patrol has had a well-defined mission which consisted of apprehension and deportation. Subsequent administrations chose to flip the script on those policies. And, in a matter of two years, transformed the border into a zone of lawlessness, with local mayors and county officials completely overwhelmed by millions of undocumented immigrants. And due to that administration's "open borders" philosophy, there appeared to be no relief in sight.

In addition to imperiling border communities, as well as large "sanctuary" cities, this open border policy also caused significant damage to the DHS employees. Not only did Border Patrol agents face greater risk to be killed or injured, but they also found themselves stretched beyond the psychological/budgetary breaking point while trying to do their jobs. This kind of policy is reckless and unsustainable.

Clearly, waiting for the next administration to (hopefully) improve the situation isn't helping matters. Instead of depending upon the whims of an upcoming President to improve/worsen the border crisis, the North American legislature will step up and solve the problem.

Congress will achieve this by first declaring zero tolerance for illegal immigration. If we are truly a nation of laws, it's vital to not reward those who break the law to enter the country. In the age of human trafficking and international terrorism, it is far too dangerous, both for the migrants as well as the Republic, to allow anyone to just wander into the country. Those who seek asylum or wish to immigrate to North America must apply for a visa outside of the NAR borders.

Second, all immigration/asylum claims will be evaluated on an individual basis. For those who wish to immigrate to North America, the Continental government will first consult each Regional Republic and see what kind of skills are most needed in their respective work forces. For those who match the needs of a particular Republic, a detailed background check of each individual's life will occur. And for the people who pass this background check, a thorough health examination will then take place. Those who are suffering from curable illnesses will get treatment. Individuals who have contracted incurable, transmittable diseases will be sent home.

Third, for those who make asylum claims, the North American government will first consider the country of origin for the asylum seeker. At which point an extremely thorough background check will occur. If the person in question passes the background check, he/she will then proceed to the health screening. This process will be codified into law by the NAR Congress. Which means that it will become the law of the land. Not a "policy" a particular President may "feel like" enforcing.

Sadly, the past few decades have demonstrated that Presidents cannot be trusted to create successful border policies. They are far too concerned about short-term political gains than the long-term security of the country. Having a clear-cut and established law concerning border security will benefit the people of North America. Border communities will experience a rebirth as lawlessness is abated, encouraging tourism and freeing them to pursue whatever social and economic policies they see fit. The large cities of the interior will also benefit, as they can dedicate their time and treasure to the communities that already live within city limits.

The various departments of DHS will also benefit from these common-sense laws. Instead of having to depend upon each administration's "interpretation" of what constitutes a secure border, the employees of DHS will be able to depend upon rock-solid, Congressional-mandated procedures every day. This will decrease burnout and make the job much safer. In the North American Republic, employees of the Border Patrol and DHS will know that they have the resources and the support of their employer. And their department will once again be held in high esteem by the representatives in D.C.

The Judicial Branch

The Judicial Branch of the federal government contains three basic levels of courts: District Courts, Circuit Courts, and the Supreme Court. In the North American system, all three levels of courts will be maintained. But there will be a modification of their jurisdiction and responsibilities.

The first level of the judicial system is the District Court. These courts are primarily used for trials of those accused of federal crimes. They also handle civil cases, bankruptcy issues, and civil suits that arise between people of different States. There are ninety-four federal District Courts throughout the United States and its territories.

The second level of the federal judiciary is Circuit Court. These are also known the United States Courts of Appeals. The Circuit Courts handle appeals from all courts beneath them; District Courts, State Courts, and Local Courts. It's important to note that Circuit Courts only hear appeals (both civil and criminal) from lower courts; they do not try any new cases. The United States features thirteen Circuit Courts, with each "Circuit" consisting of a handful of mostly contiguous States.

The third level of the federal judicial system is the US Supreme Court. It is the highest court in the land. The Supreme Court hears appeals from all lower courts. This includes District Courts, Circuit Courts, and all State and local courts. It's important to note that the US Supreme Court does not try any new cases. It only hears appeals (both civil and criminal) from lower courts.

The Supreme Court, located in Washington D.C., has become the "final stop" for all appeals cases in the country. And since the High Court has the power to judge the Constitutionality of all local, State and federal laws, it can overturn all such laws. As such, the Court has, through its power as final arbiter, ended up making law from the bench. These *de facto* laws often cover some of the most controversial topics in American life; including issues like abortion, gun control, and gay marriage.

As the United States continues to grow more diverse, politically and culturally, these Supreme Court rulings become increasingly problematic. The best-known example being Roe vs. Wade (1973), which made abortion legal throughout the country...even in States that had, through their legislatures, prohibited the procedure. This act of overriding State legislatures to enact a federal abortion law was quite controversial. And only served to divide the people from one another.

Another example is *Bush vs. Gore* (2000). The American Presidential Election of 2000 featured a very tight race. George W. Bush was challenging then Vice President Al Gore. The election ultimately came down to the State of Florida. Initially, it appeared Bush had won Florida by about a thousand votes. Due to such a small margin of victory, the Florida Supreme Court ordered a recount of all "under-vote" ballots. These ballots were not fully counted by tabulation machines, either because voters intentionally left the Presidential Election slot blank, or because of machine error. The total number of these ballots was roughly 61,000, which was more than enough to clarify the absolute winner of the election in the State.

Attorneys for George W. Bush appealed Florida's decision to the US Supreme Court. They claimed that Florida could not recount all 61,000 votes in the same manner, as urban counties in Florida used a different tabulation machine than did rural counties. This machine discrepancy, they claimed, violated the US Constitution's Equal Protection Clause, and therefore made the recount unconstitutional. The US Supreme Court agreed, and overruled Florida's decision to hold a recount. This decision essentially handed George W. Bush the Presidency.

The Supreme Court's tendency to override State legislatures and courts, as well as creating new laws, has effectively made the court a second federal legislature. This is a significant problem. Mainly because this violates the US Constitution, which only provides federal legislative power to the US Congress. But also because Supreme Court Justices are not elected by (or accountable to) the people.

It's a fact that the Supreme Court was never designed to be a legislative body. And it was not configured to dictate social policy for the entire nation. The overriding of State laws as well as the establishment of nation-wide social policy represent an encroachment upon the Rights of the American peoples. In the North American government, the Supreme Court, as well as the entire federal court system, will be returned to a state of balance. And this will be accomplished by adjusting the jurisdiction of these courts. These adjustments will be quite subtle. But their effects will be beneficial for all Americans.

At the District Court level, the changes will hardly be noticeable. Because all District Courts will retain the same basic functions in the Continental system as they do in the federal system. This includes trials for people charged with Continental crimes like counterfeiting, mail fraud, and human trafficking, as well as civil trials between people from differing States. District Courts will also be the locale for lawsuits between States.

Additionally, it will be at the District Court level that lawsuits between regions will occur. Because it's inevitable that the Regional Republics will, from time to time, have disagreements of their own. So, for example, if the Western Republic and Pacifica have a dispute over water rights, and the two Republics cannot settle their differences through negotiation, the dispute would be resolved in District Court.

Further, lawsuits between States/Regions and the Continental Government will also originate at the District Court level. It's to be expected that occasional disputes between the North American government and the States/Regions will occur. Such disagreements that cannot be negotiated successfully between the two parties will go to District Court.

It's important to note that all verdicts from the District Court can be appealed to the next highest level, the Circuit Court. This is a continuation of the current federal system. And an important one at that. Because it's at the Circuit Court that the most notable change in the federal judicial system will occur.

In the North American Republic, Circuit Courts will only hear appeals from District Courts. In other words, Circuit Courts will no longer hear appeals from local or State Courts. This move helps to prevent the rampant overreach we've seen from the Supreme Court. The most egregious Supreme Court decisions have originated from local and State courts. The removal of said cases from the Continental System stops said cases from reaching the High Court. And thereby prevents the Supreme Court from further usurpation of Constitutional authority.

There are roughly 40,000 appeals filed in Circuit Court each year.[xv] This streamlining process will help reduce that number, namely by preventing mass backlogs of cases from lower courts. This will help to ensure Americans receive fair and speedy trials... something that, sadly enough, does not occur at any level of the judicial system. It's important to note that all Circuit Court decisions can be appealed to the Supreme Court.

In the new system, the Supreme Court will remain the Highest Court in the land. But its jurisdiction will change. Instead of hearing appeals from all the lower courts in the country, the Supreme Court will only hear appeals from US District Courts and Circuit Courts.

This means that the High Court will remain the final authority on cases concerning violations of North American law, the constitutionality of Continental government actions, suits between individuals and the Continental government, issues relating to lawsuits between Regions, cases between Regions/States and the North American government, as well as suits between individuals in differing States. But its ability to meddle in State affairs, as well as its penchant for creating "one-size fits all" social policies from the bench, will be over.

Concerns

The most immediate concern about federal court modernization is its impact on civil liberties. Though the Supreme Court's public image has undergone a significant downgrade over the past decade, many people have come to view the High Court as the final guarantor of civil liberties for ordinary Americans. With the Supreme Court removed from the bulk of State and local issues, some may ask: Who will safeguard the people's Constitutional Rights?

Answer: The people themselves.

As federal court modernization takes place, a new layer of appeals courts will be created in each State. These appellate courts will be Statewide in their reach and feature judges that are elected by the people. This additional level of appeals will hear all cases that originate in local and State courts. And will act as an extra layer of protection for the peoples' civil liberties.

Having the judges of these new appeals courts elected by the people ensures that said judges are accountable to the people. And, equally important, establishing this extra layer of appellate courts at the local level will ensure that the decisions rendered from the bench represent the will of the people within each State...and not un-elected Justices from Washington D.C.

It's here that the political pluralities/minorities of each State will have their greatest affect. Because this additional layer of appellate court judges will be elected by the people, those who do not side with the State's dominant political party will serve as hedge against any potential excesses. In a representative government, it pays to have dissenting voices. And nowhere are these voices more important than in the justice system.

In addition to each State setting up an extra layer of appellate courts, each Region may choose to create their own layer of appeals courts. This will, of course, depend upon the political philosophies of the States that comprise each Regional Republic. The more collectivist Regions will doubtlessly arrange such new courts. Traditional and individualistic Regions will not.

Federal court modernization will have many benefits to the people of North America. First and foremost, it will return the focus of the Supreme Court to national-level, Constitutional issues. And put an end to the High Court's tendency to legislate from the bench. Second, court modernization will provide improved accountability to the people. Namely by adding an additional layer of appellate courts that are directly responsible to the voters. Third, court modernization will transfer the location of said appeals courts from far-flung D.C. and bring them much closer to home, where they will better reflect the will of the people.

Other Areas of Concern in North American Government

The United States Post Office

Maintaining an effective Post Office is one of the most basic functions of a modern nation. Yet for years the federal government's relationship with the US Post Office has been, at best, disingenuous. And at worst, flat-out abusive.

Every decade or so, it seems, we are told of the need to "save" the Post Office from alleged mismanagement or cost overruns. Sadly, the federal government never reveals the fact that it has stolen over $75 Billion from the Post Office.[xvi] This is because in the 1970s the USPS became a semi-independent federal agency. As part of that move, the Post Office agreed to help fund the federal employee retirement system. And the federal government has been overcharging the USPS contribution to that fund every year since then.

The first step to getting the Post Office into a place of balance is to refund the $75 billion the federal government has pilfered from it since the 1970s. Once this occurs, the North American government will sit down with USPS leadership and explore various methods to guarantee the Post Office's long-term competitiveness and stability.

Amtrak

Amtrak provides passenger rail service throughout the United States. Formed in 1971 as the National Railroad Passenger Corporation, Amtrak is a quasi-public corporation.[xvii] This means that it operates as a corporation, but is ultimately responsible to the Executive Branch and the US Congress. Between twenty and thirty million customers utilize Amtrak each year.

Although nationwide service is available, most passengers travel less than 400 miles each trip. And they usually travel from one urban area to another. In the North American Republic, Amtrak will remain a very important component of government. Top priority will be placed on high-speed rail between urban areas, the continued evolution of environmentally friendly propulsion systems, and the improvement of rail infrastructure throughout the continent.

5 ECONOMICS

One of the most basic questions to be asked of any government is: "How are we going to pay for this?" Typically, politicians will begin their answer with a discussion of taxes. But beginning there misses the point of the question. And, more importantly, ignores the fundamental problems facing the American economy.

The economy of the United States has come to the end of its road. So, before any discussion of taxes can occur, one must first begin to rebuild the American economy into something durable, sustainable, and beneficial to the American peoples. Only then can the government's role in relation to the economy be discussed.

Energy

Energy is the foundation for every economy. This is because everything in the modern world requires energy. Whether it be the movement of goods and people, the planting/harvesting of crops, or even the transmission of ideas, all modern societies run on energy.

Fortunately for us, the United States is blessed with abundant natural resources. To be clear, we have all the oil and gas we will ever need, right here in America. We've also been endowed with vast swaths of other natural energy sources, such as solar, wind, and hydroelectric power. The North American Republic will utilize all these resources. And make inexpensive energy the foundation of our New Economy.

This will start with lowering the price of gasoline. Because so much of our economy is based on transport, the NAR will prioritize lowering the cost of gasoline to an average of $1.50 to $1.75 per gallon (using today's value of the dollar). This relatively low cost of gas will help to lower prices across the board for everyday goods throughout North America.

One of the key ways to facilitate lowering the cost of gasoline is to increase domestic production of oil. This increased production will be utilized to stabilize domestic prices first, with the remainder to be sold to our friends and allies at attractive prices. The second half of this equation is to remove the federal government's "biofuels" requirement from major oil refineries.

The biofuel policy requires that corn ethanol be added to gasoline to (theoretically) reduce air pollution. These requirements have largely proven useless in terms of positive environmental impacts, with some arguing that mandates to use corn as a fuel source have done more damage to the earth (via increased use of fertilizers, water pollution, and overall emissions) than simply using gasoline. Additionally, adding corn ethanol to gasoline lowers fuel efficiency and has been known to damage vital auto parts such as engines and catalytic converters.

It's projected that forty percent of US corn production is used to make ethanol.[xviii] With the elimination of the biofuel mandate, this extra corn can feed Americans who do not have enough to eat.

For reference, the United States produced 347 million metric tons of corn in the 2022/2023 season.[xix] By removing the ethanol fuel requirement, the United States will have an extra 139 million metric tons of corn to provide to the homeless, food centers, churches, and needy Americans. Meaning no one in North America will go hungry.

The removal of the useless biofuels requirement will also allow for the construction of new refineries in North America. These new refineries, which will be strategically located away from major population centers and wildlife areas, will be built with the latest and cleanest technology we have at our disposal. In exchange for the removal of the biofuels mandate, the federal government will add a reasonable 3% charge to all oil products sold to our international friends and allies. This income will go to the general fund of the North American Congress.

This increased production and refinement capacity for oil and gas will be paired with major modernization of the national power grid. All infrastructure will be hardened against weather issues (as well as man-made attacks). This modernization will make the North American power grid the safest and most efficient energy infrastructure on the planet.

Further, the continental grid, which is currently split into three grids, will be divided into a total of six sections. This is to allow each Regional Republic its own independent grid. It's important to note that these subdivisions will not separate one Republic's infrastructure from the others, but will allow each grid to operate independently. So, if one regional grid experiences disruptions, neighboring Republics can dispatch excess power to the affected Region.

In addition to increasing oil and gas production, the North American government will continue to leverage all other natural sources of energy. This means wind, solar, hydroelectric and geothermal energy. These renewables will continue to be developed to supplement traditional methods of energy production. Equally as important, advanced/experimental methods will also be explored and developed. In short, the NAR will leverage all natural sources of energy to make life (and the environment) better for the American people.

Finally, the production of Liquefied Natural Gas (LNG) will continue to be a top priority of the NAR. In 2023, the United States became the leading exporter of LNG in the world. But this exporting, while great for business, has had an unfortunate effect of raising prices domestically.

Because of increased demand from Europe, there is less supply available to the people of the United States. And whenever supply is limited, prices rise. Seeing that North America's LNG capacity is expected to double by 2027[xx], the NAR government will institute a modest 3% increase of taxes on all LNG exports. Since it is US policies which have created such robust foreign markets, this is only fair. All tax proceeds from LNG will go towards the general fund of the North American Republic budget.

These investments in our energy infrastructure will boost the economy, create thousands of new jobs, and improve the day-to-day lives of the American peoples.

Transportation

A fully-functional economy relies on affordable energy. But it also requires quick and effective means of transportation. In North America, safe and reliable transportation will be a top priority. The Continental Congress will work diligently to build new methods of transport. And maintain what we already have.

One of the more exciting developments in 21st century transportation will be high-speed rail links between urban centers. These projects will be available in all six Regions. The Continental Congress will offer matching funds to States/Regions who wish to participate. The new rail systems will be based on the highly successful "bullet trains" from Japan. With these environmentally-friendly electric trains, it will be possible for ground travel between urban areas to safely occur at speeds of 200 miles per hour. This will drastically shorten travel time for people and products moving from one city to another.

Speaking of urban areas, the NAR will also work diligently to Unclog and Unsmog the big cities of North America. Electric Vehicles (EVs) will be promoted for those who only drive within large urban centers. The bulk of investments, however, will be put into Hybrid Vehicles (HVs). Hybrid Vehicles will be promoted for trucking as well as passenger vehicles. This advanced hybrid technology will drastically improve fuel efficiency while, at the same time, allowing for gasoline-only performance during times of power-outage or crisis.

The NAR will also develop new forms of transportation. Advances in short-range vehicle/aircraft have begun producing working prototypes of cars that can take off and land vertically, and fly for a range of over one-hundred miles. These prototypes have already received FAA approval for utilizing local airspace. Once developed to the consumer stage, these Aerial Passenger Vehicles (APVs) will offer travelers the opportunity to avoid the traffic jams of the freeways...and commute to work in the sky.

Of course, this breakthrough method of transportation will require new laws, regulations, and certifications from the States. The writer has full confidence that the people of each State and Region are up to the task.

North America's transportation infrastructure will allow for quick and efficient movement of people and goods. This safe and rapid movement will assist in keeping the NAR economy the best in the world. And it will ease the burdens of the people by making transportation quicker, less costly, and better for the environment.

Supply Chains

Healthy and durable supply chains are a vital aspect of any economy. Long supply chains are more vulnerable to chaos and disruption. While shorter supply chains tend to be more efficient and reliable.

In the late 20th and early 21st centuries, the United States created the "just in time" (JIT) supply chain. This was a system based on anticipation; where raw materials and finished goods arrived at their destinations right before they were needed. As a result, there was little to no stored inventory to be taxed. And equally as important, waste was kept to a bare minimum.

When conditions are ideal, this JIT system is truly a marvel of human ingenuity. Even if supply chains stretch thousands of miles, and cross numerous international borders, goods are available for purchase as desired. Raw materials get processed only when needed, and finished goods arrive at their destination either right before, or immediately after they are ordered. Unfortunately, conditions aren't always ideal.

This reliance on ideal conditions (and global supply chains) turned out to be a disaster for the United States. And the disaster was based on short-term thinking.

The US realized this truth in the 2020s, when pandemics and geopolitical standoffs resulted in severe disruptions and dysfunctions of the JIT supply chain. Goods that had been available on demand suddenly needed weeks or months of production time before they arrived. And some products disappeared altogether.

In the North American Republic, this situation will finally be addressed. Because one of the missions of the NAR is to reduce the size of supply chains across the continent. Specifically, this means that each Regional Republic will be encouraged to develop its own supply chains. And that means the people of each Republic will be encouraged to produce/sell their own goods to supplement already-existing sources.

In the early 21st century, people from across the United States are creating various products, from agricultural goods, clothing, art, jewelry, etc., and selling these items online. These homemade goods and foodstuffs then get shipped throughout America. The NAR government will encourage and nurture this type of behavior across every State and Region.

This entrepreneurial spirit will supplement and enhance already-existing supply chains of the United States. Items that aren't readily available from international sources or large corporations will become available from "mom and pop" sellers across the continent. This will provide the people of the NAR greater choice. And will ultimately lead to both higher-quality goods and lower prices.

Additionally, this network, or "Spider's Web" of local producers, will stimulate economic activity across North America. Because the people of each State and Republic will be encouraged to create items (and form cooperatives with their friends and neighbors to do same), they will by necessity be required to purchase or grow more raw materials from their area. All of which will result in a strengthened local economy (and tax revenue on both ends the chain).

And because the entirety of the North American Republic is a free trade zone, the goods and services produced inside the NAR will move quickly across the continent. This will be especially beneficial for each of the Regional Republics. Because each Republic has certain natural or geographical advantages, some products will only be able to be manufactured inside their respective region. Thus, allowing an incredible opportunity for each Republic to sell their products with zero trade barriers. And as the North American Republic grows, so too will the potential for free trade opportunities.

Just as quick and efficient transportation will be a hallmark of the NAR, so too will be the quick and efficient movement of goods and services. So much so that the North American Republic will be viewed not only as wonder of modern political arrangement...but also as a tremendous place to do business.

Interest Rates

Developed economies are most successful when they offer their people relatively easy access to credit. When credit is expensive and/or hard to come by, economic activity grinds to a halt. This is because most people simply don't have the out-of-pocket resources to start new businesses, purchase vehicles, or buy already-constructed homes. So, when people wish to do these things, they must borrow money. Unfortunately, in the United States, there is very little protection for the consumer when it comes to usury.

The most common form of credit in the US is the **credit card**. Indeed, the use of credit cards inside America has exploded in the past three decades. And rightly so, as credit cards offer a fast, convenient, and relatively safe way to complete transactions. Sadly, the typical interest rate for credit cards hovers around thirty percent. Meaning that if a consumer misses a monthly payment, he or she can expect to pay thirty percent on top of the balance owed.

Because of these astronomical interest rates, once they miss a payment or two, most Americans find it impossible to ever get out of this kind of debt. This is evidenced by the over $1 Trillion of credit card debt carried by Americans at the time of publication.[xxi] Obviously, this amount of debt serves as an albatross on the necks of the people. But it's also a drain on the economy of the United States. Mainly because people who are driven into huge amounts of debt don't have the buying power to purchase other items. Most of their money must go to servicing the debt. And that means economic drivers like buying cars, starting businesses, and purchasing homes are all out of the question.

Car loans are one area in which people often are victimized by usury. Although some States place a cap on how high lenders may set rates for automobile loans, it's not unheard of to see interest rates as high as thirty or forty percent! This type of predatory behavior often targets young people, as well as Black Americans, as both groups typically have fewer choices when it comes to financing their car purchases.

Home loans are another area in which the limit of interest rate is set by each State. It's not uncommon for a maximum of ten percent interest to be the legal limit for home loans in a State. Even at ten percent, however, many Americans find this level of interest to be cost-prohibitive for buying a home. But the worst example of usury for everyday Americans is the **title loan/payday loan businesses.** These hucksters can (and will) charge interest rates of between 200% - 500%! For this kind of activity to be legal anywhere in America is an absolute disgrace.

The amount of **usury** being permitted across the United States is an act of pure evil. Sadly, because the governments of the United States (Federal, State, and local) are all controlled/influenced by Big Finance, the situation is only getting worse. Americans, much like their governments, are being buried under mountains of debt. Most of which is created by excessive interest rates.

In the North American Republic, usury will be illegal in every State and Region. The maximum interest rate allowed for home and auto loans, credit cards, and title/payday loans will be five percent. The average American will never have to endure outrageous interest rates to live their everyday lives. Additionally, at the time of the adoption of the North American dollar, a debt jubilee will occur which will forgive every public and private debt inside the United States of America. This will serve as a clean break from the corrupt federal system and start everyone in the

NAR with a clean slate.

Taxes

With the above changes significantly strengthening the economy, now we can begin to discuss taxation. To be blunt: Taxes are a necessary evil. But just because they're necessary doesn't mean they have to be harsh or burdensome. The current federal income tax is a complex, jumbled mess of rules and regulations. It is, in theory, a "progressive" tax. This means that it allegedly charges lower tax rates to those who make less money, and charges higher tax rates to those who make more money. And at first glance, this appears to be true.

As of the time of publication, there are seven different federal income tax brackets. These brackets range from ten percent tax (for those making $11,000 or less) to thirty-seven percent tax (for those earning $578,126 or more). On the surface, this appears to be a reasonable way to construct a tax system. That is, until one takes a closer look.

When you look under the surface, you see that big corporations like Amazon, Nike, and HP often pay zero federal income tax. Despite each of these companies bringing in billions of dollars each year in revenue. This is allowed to occur because the federal government has written numerous breaks for mega-corporations directly into the tax code. Unfortunately, there are no such tax breaks for the average American.

The United States federal government has purposely created this two-tiered tax system. The first system is designed for the benefit of the wealthy and the corporations. The second system is designed for everybody else. And, quite incredibly, under that two-tiered system, schoolteachers and mechanics will end up paying more federal taxes than mega corporations. This kind of corruption cannot stand.

In North America, the two-tiered tax system will be thrown

out. Since corporations have been declared, in the eyes of the courts, to be the same as individuals, then they will be subject to the same tax rates as individuals. In short, the days of the mega corporations shirking their tax duty will be over. And, for the first time in many decades, a fair tax will be implemented. The NAR Fair Tax will be both progressive and flat. In that it will charge no income tax to those making less than $20,000 per year (current value). And for people making $50,000 or more, the tax will be a flat 13%.

This accomplishes two goals: First, it protects those earning modest incomes. People who are beginning their work journey (or starting over) often-times must accept lower-paying jobs. This new tax system allows those who are working low-paying jobs to keep all their income. This will help free up money for necessities like food, housing, car notes, childcare, and education. Second, the NAR system provides *everyone* with a significant tax break. In these challenging times, every dollar counts. And the North American Republic will make sure that everyone has more money in their pockets.

As the table below illustrates, those making less than $20,000 per year pay no tax. The flat 13% tax begins for a single person making $50,000 or more. For those earning incomes between those two amounts, taxes begin at 1% and grow as income increases. ***It's important to note that, due to inflation, the starting point of this new tax plan can be moved up as high as $50,000.***

Income	Total Tax
$20,000-$22,000	1%
$23,000-$25,000	2%
$26,000-$29,000	3%
$30,000-$32,000	4%
$33,000-$34,000	5%
$35,000-$36,000	6%
$37,000-$38,000	7%
$39,000-$40,000	8%
$41,000-$42,000	9%
$43,000-$44,000	10%
$45,000-$46,000	11%
$47,000-$49,000	12%
$50,000 +	13%

The Regions

The federal government's current tax system closely resembles a black hole. When money goes into D.C., it completely disappears. And where it goes, no one knows.

Under the Continental system, the States will determine how 1/3 of all income taxes are spent. This is because each Regional Republic will receive approximately one-third of the income taxes collected from the people of their member States. This money will go directly into the general fund of each Regional government. And the people of each State will determine how their Regional government spends this money.

This factor is of great importance. Inside the federal system, States have little influence on where income tax money goes. And quite frankly, once the money gets to DC, nobody really knows what goes where. Under the Continental system, the States will determine how 1/3 of all income taxes are spent. This provides the people with greater accountability for their tax dollars. And greater control over where these funds go.

So, in the new system, every single American will receive a tax break. And, under the NAR tax plan, the people of the States (via their Regional governments) will determine how 1/3 of all income taxes are to be spent. This means that Americans be taxed less, and they will have greater control over where their tax dollars are going.

This is a win/win outcome. And very typical of the laws and policies of the Continental system. That's because the North American Republic is built for the benefit of the people. And the above economic changes demonstrate that fact.

The amount of economic potential on this continent is truly amazing. The above changes will go a long way towards unlocking that potential. And, more importantly, these changes will make life much easier for the people of North America.

6 SOCIAL ISSUES

Social issues are some of the most challenging aspects of the 21st century. Everywhere, it seems, people want to discuss, debate, and argue about topics like abortion, gun control, and gender. And due to the current federal system's "one size fits all" approach, the size and ramifications of these debates tend to get out of control very quickly.

Fortunately, the North American system addresses most of these issues through its Regional Republics. The States that comprise each Regional Republic decide how to handle these issues, and then coordinate their responses within their respective regions. Because of this, tensions over social issues remain very low. In North America, there's always a State/Region that aligns with your personal beliefs.

Understanding this, there are still issues, inherited via the previous federal systems, that remain unresolved. As such, these key social issues need to be addressed by the North American government from the beginning.

Black Americans

Black Americans are a unique people. Through incredible privations and ill treatment, they have persevered to form their own ethnic group inside of Western Culture. Black America features a shared history, its own approach to language, religion and politics, and a signature culture that has influenced all the nations of the globe.

In the federal system, the government's approach to Black America has been to keep the bulk of the people poor and living in urban areas. This makes for a relatively easily controlled population that can be relied upon for votes in local elections. The federal system is especially fond of highlighting Black America's historical injustices and hardships, and then harnessing the subsequent anger for political purposes. This is accompanied by vague promises of "equality", which are never actually achieved, but forever remain something to be accomplished in the future. Namely through protests, marches, and continued voting for progressive urban candidates.

The result is a rather depressing hamster wheel. In which Black Americans are continually placed at the back of the line, economically, socially, and politically. All while being abused by unjust laws and unfair economic policies. After a particularly gruesome example of this unfair treatment is captured on video (usually via an encounter with law enforcement), the Black Community is then provoked into a rage by the media and political establishment. Demonstrations, protests, and occasional riots ensue. The outrage from this situation is then harnessed into supporting candidates who once again place the Black Community at the back of the line. Thus, allowing the cycle to repeat itself, indefinitely.

In North America, the Black Community will finally be able to lift itself from this vicious cycle. Instead of relegating the community into perpetual poverty and victimhood, the North American Republic will honor Black Americans' unique culture. And this empowerment will not just come in the form of words. Because North America will do something the federal system has failed to accomplish: provide Black Americans a land of their own.

A Black Autonomous Zone (BAZ) will be created within the Republic. It will feature good-quality land with multiple natural advantages. Socially, it will be a safe space that features Black mayors, police chiefs, bank presidents, principals, and pastors. Politically, this zone will offer Black Americans something that they've never truly had: freedom.

This means the freedom to chart their own course of development. No longer will Black America be used as a pawn of the two-party system. Because in the Black Autonomous Zone, the development of Black Culture will depend entirely upon the will and desire of Black Americans. It's important to note that, as with all other States/Regions of the North American Republic, Equal Protection under the law is the law of the land. And this applies to the Black Autonomous Zone as well. The BAZ will certainly be a predominantly Black entity, but this does not mean that other groups can be banned or treated differently.

The size and scope of the Black Autonomous Zone will be determined by leadership of the Black Community, the North American Republic, as well as the States and Regional Republics. However the specifics are decided, the result will be a win-win outcome for the people of North America.

The Black Community was nominally emancipated in 1865. Since that point in time, Black America has found itself re-chained to abysmal schools, decaying urban centers, and terrible economic conditions. Now is the time to right those wrongs. And the Black Autonomous Zone will go a long way towards accomplishing that goal.

Native Americans

Native Americans are the most impoverished people in the United States. The main culprit for this situation is that tribes do not have control over their allotted lands. Instead, the federal government deems the American Indians to be leaseholders, and, as such, exerts excessive controls on what can and cannot take place on Tribal lands.[xxii]

This means that even everyday functions, such as buying a house, result in unnecessary red tape and higher mortgage rates. That extraordinary level of bureaucracy also extends to business ventures like oil and gas exploration. Where it's estimated that Native Americans are required to submit over ten times the amount of permitting paperwork compared to the States.

This type of regulatory stranglehold on Native American lands is cruel and unnecessary. The North American government will work to rapidly level the playing field. Namely, by turning over ownership of Native lands to their respective tribes, and equalizing federal laws for economic activities occurring inside of tribal lands. This will result in the Tribes owning their land outright. And any business they wish to do will require the same amount of paperwork as business occurring in the States.

Additionally, the North American government will review each treaty inherited from the current federal government. A top priority will be placed on the NAR bringing each active treaty with the various Tribes into a state of full adherence.

Generation Z (And the Young Millennials)

The abandonment of Generation Z is one of the most depressing chapters of the modern era. This entire generation of young people has been left in the lurch by a non-functioning government, failing social institutions, and a collapsing economy. They, along with their elders from the Millennial Generation, are perhaps the most tragic victims of the current age.

All the promises of American society have been shattered during their youth: Going to college and earning a degree doesn't guarantee a decent job will follow. Home ownership may not be affordable, even to those who have decent jobs. Working hard and playing by the rules could result in abject failure. The next generation of children will likely be financially less well-off than their parents. And when confronted with these abysmal truths, the only solution our current leaders can offer is to say, "Pull yourself up by your bootstraps, kid!". Unfortunately for the youth, when they pull themselves up, there's nothing to see but broken promises.

The North American Republic will address the abandonment of the youth in three ways: First, there will be real jobs available as the NAR builds and improves North American infrastructure. These jobs will focus on a plethora of specializations, from planning and research and design to construction and labor. Meaning that those who are looking for work can find employment in a variety of fields.

Second, employees of the NAR Infrastructure team will receive one year of education credits for each year on the job (up to four years). These credits will allow each worker to continue his or her education in the field of their choice. Workers may opt to study a field they experienced directly as part of the infrastructure team. Or they may try their hands at a completely new area of specialization. These fields of study will include areas that are of the most pressing need for the remainder of the century. Which means that there's a high likelihood of jobs being available after studies in said fields are completed.

Third, first-time home and car buyers will receive notable tax credits for their initial year of ownership. An individual's first car or home is often a watershed moment in life. The North American Republic encourages its peoples to accomplish these kinds of milestones, regardless of age. These tax breaks will benefit everyone. Most notably the young people of North America. The current system's abandonment of Generation Z (as well as young Millennials) is a shameful act. The North American Republic will reverse this bad policy and preserve and strengthen this generation from day one.

Practical Environmentalism

Environmentalism, like so many other aspects of American life, has become completely politicized. This is an unfortunate development, to say the least. Because basic, common-sense environmentalism benefits us all.

Sadly, the current "green" movement has been hijacked by people using environmental concerns as a pretext for human population reduction. This is given away by their obsession with reducing the amount of "carbon" on the planet. Typically, these hucksters will declare a date, usually ten-to-twenty years in the future, in which the world will be facing apocalyptic conditions. These catastrophes, they say, can only be prevented by reducing the amount of carbon on the planet.

What's implicit in this statement is that humans (and animals) are carbon-based creatures. Thus, what the so-called greens are truly saying is that they want most people to be eliminated. One can hear this message repeated in a variety of ways. It may come in the guise of discouraging people from having children, the support of no-holds-barred euthanasia, the elimination of household pets like cats and dogs, and even the cessation of farming. But regardless of what form these soundbites take, the basic message is always the same: You need to die to save the planet.

The fact that the chief proponents of this message fail to lead by example is telling.

The North American Republic's approach to the subject is different. Its foundation rests on the great truth that human beings are an indispensable part of the environment. We all are born into and come from the earth. As such, the earth is home for all of us. And as sentient creatures, it is our responsibility to act as good stewards; to manage our resources wisely, to curtail pollution and waste, and to invest time and money into making sure our home is safe and clean for future generations. Practical

Environmentalism does just that. And it accomplishes this by prioritizing resources to the most egregious, immediate threats to our environment. In other words, by putting out the biggest fires first.

For example, the dumping of nuclear waste into the Pacific Ocean (via the Fukushima reactor) is an immediate and serious concern. Not only for the peoples of North America, but for everyone in the world.[xxiii] Yet few, if any, environmentalists are discussing it. The poisoning of the world's largest ocean (and much of our food supply) will have ramifications upon this planet for hundreds, if not thousands, of years.

Domestically, there are significant problems as well. Drinking water contamination in cities like Flint, Michigan, and Jackson, Mississippi, continues to plague residents in those areas.[xxiv] The fact that these problems have become chronic (even generational) tells one all they need to know about the state of environmentalism in America.

The North American government will address each of these issues. For international problems like the Fukushima nuclear waste release, the NAR will partner with the nations of the Pacific and utilize the very best technology available to solve the problem. By combining the resources of nations like Japan, Australia, Russia, India, and China, as well as North America, we can begin to not only remit the problem of radioactivity in the Pacific, but also to prevent similar events from ever happening again.

For domestic emergencies, such as the water crises of Michigan and Mississippi, the NAR government will leverage the best and brightest minds from across the continent. This includes individuals from the water treatment industry, and also from universities and colleges across the Republic. Those who create the most innovative and efficient solutions will receive grant funding for future research. And these solutions (as well as the tools necessary to implement them) will be presented to the State and local governments so they can solve the problems for good.

Less immediate concerns will be addressed by a combination of efficiency and wise planning. A wonderful example is reducing automobile emissions. There are a multitude of ways to achieve this goal. First, the continued development of hybrid technology will reduce the amount of pollutants emitted by cars and long-haul trucks across the continent. Second, the NAR will encourage urban commuters to consider electric vehicles to decrease pollution in our cities. Third, the NAR government will push the automobile industry to achieve efficiency standards of 50 miles per gallon by 2030. These initiatives will go a long way towards reducing emissions and making North America the cleanest continent in the world.

Another way to cleanse the environment is to put a stop to practices that do more harm than good. For example, spraying sulfur dioxide into the atmosphere will be prohibited across the North American Republic. This practice, which is currently taking place at various locations in the United States, involves injecting the toxic chemical into the stratosphere to reduce atmospheric heat.[xxv] Sadly, any theoretical benefits achieved by this procedure are outweighed by its deadly consequences.

Sulfur dioxide is extremely hazardous to human and animal life. It's also the same substance produced by coal plants and volcanoes. Sulfur dioxide poisons the respiratory systems of humans as well as animals. And once released into the air, the toxic chemical eventually comes back down to earth, in the form of acid rain. This sulfuric acid rain then damages plant life, marine animals, insects, ocean waters, lakes, rivers, soil, forests, and drinking water. Obviously, destroying all life on Earth is not a sound environmental policy. The maniacs who advocate injecting deadly poisons into our atmosphere to "save the planet" will be out of a job on the first day of the NAR.

Instead of injecting death into the skies, the North American Republic will plant life into the ground. Namely, by the act of reforestation. Trees are nature's "scrubbers", in that they absorb carbon dioxide from the atmosphere and release oxygen. This kind of air purification, especially in our modern world, is priceless.

In addition to cleaning the air, trees also help prevent soil erosion, reduce urban heat, act as flood barriers, and provide food for humans and wildlife.[xxvi] Understanding these immense benefits, the NAR will advocate for continual "Arbor Drives" in which trees are planted on all Continental lands. Resources to do the same will be provided to each of the States and Regional Republics. Private citizens will also have access to these resources.

Utilizing clean energy sources will be another key aspect of North America's plans. Currently, alternative energy (wind, solar, hydro, & thermal) accounts for about twenty percent of total US power production. The NAR government will advocate for increased usage of renewables. It's important to note that this support depends on making clean power sources as cost-effective and reliable as traditional methods.

Finally, North America will continue to develop emerging technology for continental, regional, and local use. This new technology will represent amazing breakthroughs in energy, transportation, and environmental repair. The technological developments that are coming will stretch the limits of what many thought was humanly possible. It's up to us to make sure these advancements are used for the good of the people and the planet.

Animal Rights

Humans are the stewards of the earth. And this means it is our responsibility to care for all the living, breathing things on this planet. Ultimately, the level of care we display to these creatures will reflect back to humanity.

Unfortunately, the track record of humane treatment of

animals has not always been good. As recently as 2022, it was reported that the chief medical advisor to the US President was approving hundreds of thousands of dollars in federal funds for cruel experiments in which dogs were drugged and/or infested with deadly insects. These canines, some of them as young as six-month-old puppies, had their vocal cords severed so their yelps of pain could not be heard as they were consumed by these insects.[xxvii]

This kind of sadistic behavior serves no scientific purpose. That's why the North American Republic will ban such senseless and cruel treatment of animals. Under the NAR government, animal testing will be curtailed to only the most vital cases. And absolutely no Continental Government funds will go to laboratories that support barbaric practices against animals.

Another key NAR priority will be the promotion of humane livestock procedures. The Continental Government, working with private entities, will make funds available to farmers and ranchers in every State and Regional Republic to convert their acreage into cage-free and free-range properties. This conversion process will be provided at no cost to ranchers and farmers who wish to participate.

Finally, the North American government will prohibit euthanizing animals for population control purposes. There are times, of course, when an animal is terminally ill and suffering, or, less frequently, when an animal attacks and kills a human. In such cases, euthanasia is appropriate. But the termination of animal life merely for population control reasons is not appropriate and will be prohibited on every bit of Continental Government property.

Vulnerable Populations

There's an adage that says a civilization can be judged by how it treats its most vulnerable. In the United States, vulnerable populations tend to get placed last in line. This is a source of immeasurable shame for our society. In North America, every person will be treated as a valuable member of the community. And that means the most vulnerable will be placed at the front of the line.

Many States have begun the process of re-confirming their support for the unborn. This is an admirable goal. That support, however, often ends after the child is born. And from that point, the States who fought so hard to protect the lives of the unborn turn a blind eye to the suffering of the children they become.

In the Republic, our commitment to children isn't cut with the umbilical cord. The NAR government will fight to make sure that every child has a decent and safe home, with adequate food, healthcare, and educational opportunities. This means extra resources will be made available to the States and Regions to accomplish these goals. Additionally, those who willingly harm the young by trafficking children into North America will face severe punishments and mandatory prison time.

The elderly are equally important. For far too long, our society has treated elders as disposable burdens. Horrifically, some have even called for people who reach a certain age to be killed off in the name of "population control". The NAR takes the opposite stance: Every citizen, regardless of age or medical condition, is of great value to our society.

As such, the NAR will encourage the States and Republics to maintain the best level of care available for their elderly citizens. This will be accomplished by continued support of what is now known as Medicare. The North American government will also provide tax breaks to all citizens who open their homes to elderly relatives. Finally, the Continental Government will recommend to the States that all those who wish to become nurses spend one year (preferably during nursing school) working at hospice and/or retirement homes.

The United States made great strides in caring for and

assisting the disabled. It is to the credit of the federal system that laws such as the Americans with Disabilities Act (ADA) were created. The NAR will continue to uphold this level of commitment to our disabled citizens. And we will strive to develop emerging technologies to assist those who are struggling with disabilities.

Veterans are another key area of concern for North America. Those who put their lives on the line for the United States often return home and suffer from neglect. And this neglect transforms into anger, hopelessness, and depression. As recently as 2021, seventeen veterans commit suicide each day in the United States.[xxviii] This is simply unacceptable.

Instead of adopting the federal system's habit of working backwards, the Continental Government will utilize a forward-thinking approach. Namely, by asking a simple question: What are veterans experiencing that causes so many of them to commit suicide after returning home? It would be wise to start suicide prevention strategies by reviewing the actions each veteran was asked to perform while in uniform. And, if a connection can be found linking these actions to suicidal ideation, to change those actions for future service men and women.

This approach is to be combined with increased funding from the Continental Government for therapy, as well as re-integration assistance, for those who are discharged from the service. The days of drugging the problem away are over. Our veterans give their all for this country. It's only right that we do the same for them when they return home.

The less fortunate of North America will also be a top priority. Currently, 38 million Americans fall below the poverty line in the United States.[xxix] This means that one in ten citizens do not have enough to eat, or access to decent healthcare. The triad approach of food, healthcare, and skills will be employed to ease the burdens of the poor.

For food needs, the NAR government will work with food

pantries, shelters, and places of worship to continue to distribute foodstuffs to the less fortunate. Currently, the federal government makes direct food donations through programs like The Emergency Food Assistance Program (TEFAP), the Commodity Supplemental Food Program (CSFP), and the Women's Infants and Children (WIC) program. These programs provide over four billion meals to the American people each year.[xxx] All these programs will continue at current levels. These food donations will be buttressed by an additional 139 million metric tons of corn each year. This extra food will be available because of North America ending the federal government's biofuels requirement. These combined programs will provide food to each person in need, in every State of the Republic.

To help the less fortunate with healthcare, a variety of approaches will be utilized. This includes Medicare, the use of vouchers and tax credits for health maintenance/emergency services, as well as the newly-established Local Clinic (LC) system. This network of solutions will go a long way towards helping those in need find health services, regardless of which State or Region in which they reside.

Of equal importance to food and medical care is the opportunity to find work. Unfortunately, many Americans below the poverty line seek employment, but are denied the opportunity due to a lack of skills. The NAR will work diligently to see which fields of employment are in the greatest need of workers, and then provide these skills to the less fortunate. Additionally, those who fall below the poverty line may apply to work on the various infrastructure programs of the NAR. These projects will provide their workers with a fair wage, as well as one year of college/trade school credit for each year on the job.

Being a citizen of the North American Republic means being a valued member of society. And regardless of where one is on his/her journey, there will always be the opportunity to make a difference in their own life, as well as that of their community.

The NAR respects all and will strive to make sure each person has a full slate of opportunities at their disposal. Because an empowered citizen is much more likely to become a productive citizen. And a productive citizen is much more likely to find happiness.

7 FOREIGN RELATIONS

National Strategy

The national strategy of the United States is antiquated and non-viable. It is based on a theory, promulgated in the early 90s, that states America can dominate the world by controlling the Eurasian landmass. There are two fatal flaws to that theory.

First, the Eurasian Strategy assumes that the military superiority America enjoyed in the 1990s will last forever. A quick look at the world shows that this is not the case. Peer nations have not only caught up to US technology, but in some cases, such as the development of hypersonic missiles, have surpassed American military capabilities. As a result of these developments, America has awakened to the fact that it can no longer act with impunity on the world stage.

Additionally, non-peer nations have harnessed low-cost technology, like drones, to begin making a noticeable impact on world affairs. This includes disrupting international shipping lanes, blowing up naval and land vessels, and generally wreaking havoc on global trade. And while the US Armed Forces are more than capable of countering these non-peer actors, they often resort to using armaments that cost hundreds of thousands of dollars apiece in the process. Which means the non-peer actors are effectively using our technological superiority against us.

The second fatal flaw of the Eurasian Strategy is the assumption that America will always be able to spend unlimited amounts of money on its military. At the time of publication, the annual US defense budget is $886 Billion. The annual interest payment the government must make to service the national debt is now $870 Billion.[xxxi] This means that the government's national debt payments are now roughly equal to—and will soon exceed—its annual military budget.

As the national debt continues to rise, so will the yearly interest payments required to carry that debt. Which means that less and less money will be available for the military…and domestic programs as well. All that makes the Eurasian Strategy, as currently defined, completely untenable. The United States will not have the resources available to continue playing the role of World's Policeman.

North America's national strategy will rely upon a strong military. But a strong military, by itself, is insufficient to accomplish foreign policy goals in the new age. To be a fully-dimensional State in the 21st century, one must embrace and participate in the multi-polar world. And that means learning to utilize the full complement of tools at our disposal.

Fortunately for us, there's an abundance of available talent throughout the Continent. America features the most diverse population of individuals on the planet, with people from nearly every part of the globe. Leveraging these in-built connections, the North American Republic will work tirelessly to train and educate a new generation of ambassadors, diplomats, and representatives to engage the world, and forge positive relationships with all governments.

Unlike the United States, which utilizes a "bomb first, ask questions later" approach, the NAR will prioritize peace and stability as the main planks of our foreign policy. This means that mutually beneficial outcomes will always be the first goal of any negotiation. And that coercive force will only be used as a last resort.

Defense Posture

Every Great Power must have a strong and effective military. Fortunately, North America inherits one of the best militaries in the world via the United States. And while there are always improvements to be made to any organization, the most pressing issue isn't the strength or structure of the US Armed Forces. The main priority is the posture of our military.

To be the World's Policeman, one must have a presence in every corner of the globe. As of 2024, the United States has 750 military bases around the world. These bases stretch across eighty different countries. And the total maintenance costs of these installations are $80 Billion per year…or about $1 Trillion every twelve years.[xxxii] Most of these installations are unnecessary for the protection of our homeland.

Since 2003, the United States has spent approximately $8 Trillion on wars in Iraq, Afghanistan, and Pakistan. These conflicts have, at best, yielded inconclusive results. The "forever wars" have also resulted in an incredible loss of life: It's estimated that 15,000 US troops and contractors perished in these and other conflicts, along with 4.6 million civilians.[xxxiii] Astonishingly, over 38 million people have been unwillingly removed from their homes, with many becoming refugees flooding into places like Europe.[xxxiv]

Domestically, 52,000 veterans returned home with injuries from these wars.[xxxv] These wounds range from minor to severe, up to and including loss of limbs. There are also psychological traumas from which our veterans continue to suffer. Depression, anxiety, and Post Traumatic Stress Disorder (PTSD) have contributed to an average of seventeen veterans committing suicide each day.

Interestingly, when Americans are asked why our Armed Forces were sent into places like Iraq, Afghanistan, and Pakistan, one might hear vague responses about "freedom" or "democracy". But in terms of a real, tangible reason, no one seems to know. And when asked what benefits these wars provided the American people, the answers remain elusive.

Clearly, the time for change is upon us. America cannot afford to continue prosecuting endless wars across the globe. The financial burdens and human costs have become far too great.

This is why the North American Republic will feature an entirely new defense posture. Instead of projecting power to maintain a global empire, the NAR will prioritize defending the American homeland. And from that point, the Republic will be very selective about its defense objectives. This includes when and where we utilize our Armed Forces. This new defense posture will certainly keep America engaged with the world. The most noticeable change will be *how* we engage with the world.

International Organizations

The United Nations was formed in 1945 in San Francisco, California. Its main purpose was to prevent World War 3. The UN was also tasked to build and solidify a framework of international law, protect human rights, deliver humanitarian assistance, and, most recently, to support sustainable development and climate action.[xxxvi]

The UN was born into a world that was almost completely devastated by World War 2. At that time, the only Great Powers left standing were the United States and Soviet Union. Because of this, both superpowers got to decide how the post-war world was going to work. In that era, the planet was essentially divided into two camps: the Democratic West led by the United States, and the Communist Bloc led by the Soviet Union. Both sides made sure the bi-polar nature of the world was incorporated into the power structure of the United Nations.

This manifested most visibly in the creation of the UN Security Council (SC). The Security Council has the bulk of authority in the United Nations. The SC has the power to investigate and mediate conflicts, enact embargoes and sanctions, and instigate military action against sovereign nations. The five permanent members of the Security Council are: The United States, Great Britain, France, The Russian Federation, and China. Each of these countries has veto power over all meaningful actions of the UN. And each of these countries represents the bifurcated Democratic/Communist world of the 20th century.

It's clear that this arrangement served the planet well during the Cold War. Primarily because it helped prevent World War 3. However, as the world progresses further away from a bipolar status, and deeper into a multi-polar system, having five nations possess decision-making authority will likely instigate more problems than it solves. A modernization of the United Nations is, therefore, imperative.

The new UN will need to consider the emergence of multiple power centers around the world. The writer proposes expanding the lineup of permanent, veto-holding members of the Security Council from five to ten. This expansion will benefit Emerging Powers, provide greater representation to the peoples of the world, and, most importantly, act as a check-and-balance system for global affairs.

For example, a new SC featuring permanent members of the North American Republic, Great Britain, The European Union (France), The Russian Federation, China, India, Japan, The African Union, South America, and the Arab League would directly represent most of the peoples of the world. And more accurately reflect the diverse array of power centers around the globe.

Some may argue that the increase to ten members will make the Security Council less efficient. This writer responds by stating that sometimes it's best when the government operates with less efficiency. Because this allows more time for thinking and compromise. And less time to make knee-jerk decisions. In the high-stakes world of 21st century politics, the more thinking that we do, the more likely it is that humanity wins.

America's Role in The New World

The United States has been the main driver of international affairs for the past thirty years. Politically, economically, culturally, and militarily. Many Americans take pride in this. An equal (if not greater) number of Americans have grown weary of the endless wars that the United States has entangled itself in for the past three decades. So, the question becomes: How do we maintain a position of leadership in the world while at the same time ending the Forever Wars? The answer is simple. We rely upon our greatest strength: Our ideas.

America has, for centuries now, served as a beacon in the night for those yearning to be free. The ideals that emerged from the Declaration of Independence and the US Constitution astonished the world. Many asked how it was possible that men could govern themselves without a monarch. Later, they wondered how a system could function when citizens can speak freely of (and defend themselves from) the very government from which they swore allegiance.

Subsequent questions emerged about how a country could feature equal rights amongst men and women. And later still, how a nation could guarantee equal rights for people of every background and ethnicity. For each of these questions, America answered. Not with force of arms, but with ideas. And as we march into the 21st century, we are again called upon to lead. That doesn't mean leading the world into another Great War. But to lead by virtue of our ideas.

And that's the beauty of the multi-polar world. It is a world of great debate. It's a world in which the most complex problems in human history will be solved by those with the best ideas. In short, it's a world tailor-made for America. To those who are concerned about a loss of prestige in this new era, I can assure you that these are empty fears. The world does not want (or need) to be ruled by an iron fist. The peoples of Earth desire peace and prosperity. And through the strength of our ideals and innovation, as well as the spirit of cooperation, all nations can work together to achieve that goal.

So, does America have the courage to transform the world once again? And usher in an era of peace and prosperity? The writer believes the people of America can achieve this goal. And that the North American Republic is ready for the challenge.

8 FREQUENTLY ASKED QUESTIONS

Why Not Red States and Blue States?

One of the more frequently discussed options of the early 2020s was the "National Divorce". This divorce was to consist of a permanent separation of the United States into two countries: Red State America and Blue State America. While such an idea may sound appealing on the surface, there are numerous, substantial flaws that make such a concept non-viable.

The first flaw of the National Divorce scheme is that political parties are designed to be hostile to their rivals. The Democratic and Republican parties have gathered a great deal of attention (and money) by demonizing their opponents at every turn. This behavior is a logical way for both parties in our modern political circus. Unfortunately, it's not a logical ideology on which to build a country.

In the National Divorce scenario, hostility against the "other side" would become the dominant ideology of both nations. Unfortunately, with both political parties possessing armies, navies, and nuclear weapons. Inevitably, both countries' overriding mission would be the destruction of the opposite nation. This would manifest in either a direct confrontation, or by forming alliances with foreign powers to destroy the "Evil Red" or "Wicked Blue" America. The results would be disastrous.

A second reason why the National Divorce idea is a non-starter is that political parties are transitory; They come and go as the times change. Since the founding of the United States, parties such as the Whigs, Federalists, Democratic-Republicans, Know-Nothings, and Free-Soilers have all vanished from the scene. It's not unimaginable that one (or both) of our current parties will meet a similar fate. The fact is political parties tend to have relatively brief shelf lives. As such, they make a poor foundation for any nation.

Finally, most States have significant numbers of opposition voters living in their territory. If Red States feature large urban centers, most citizens in those areas tend to vote blue. And Blue States with rural areas often see most citizens in those locales voting red. While it's theoretically possible for everyone "trapped behind enemy lines" to pick up stakes and move, this sorting process could take years to complete. The time and money needed to make all these moves possible would waste much of the dynamic energy of the people. And would also result in complete chaos for both red and blue America.

Taking these factors into consideration, the Red/Blue "National Divorce" concept becomes a recipe for disaster. So it has been discarded in favor of a much more dynamic and practical system.

Why Not Fifty Republics?

Though less popular than the "Red/Blue" concept, some have wondered why we don't just disband the federal government and make each State its own Republic. There are numerous reasons why this strategy wouldn't be viable.

First, only a handful of States are financially sound. A look at the "Donor/Receiver" States from 2022 shows that nearly half of the States take more money from the federal government than they send.[xxxvii] In the event of a sudden disbanding of the national government, these States would automatically find themselves in financial trouble.

Second, having half of the States on the continent becoming financially insolvent represents a substantial security risk. A State that teeters on the verge of economic collapse often becomes desperate, and open to the influences of the highest bidder. Many of those high bidders will be foreign governments looking to encroach upon North American territory. This is an intolerable outcome. And one that would come to fruition if the fifty States suddenly found themselves completely independent.

A third issue is the ever-present threat of emergencies and disasters. Even economic powerhouses like California and Texas will encounter earthquakes, hurricanes, and other destructive acts of nature. When these occur, it's best to have someone to turn to for assistance. Having the safety net of a regional and continental government helps to improve both the quality and timeliness of such a response.

Why Not a North American "Union"?

Some have suggested the way out of our current mess is to combine the United States, Mexico, and Canada into one large political unit. Of all the above scenarios, this is by far the worst. The peoples of the United States, Mexico, and Canada are currently suffering from unrepresentative and corrupt governments. The "merger" of the three countries would only compound these issues.

Primarily because lack of representation is already a severe problem. Currently, each member of the US House represents, on average, about 760,000 people.[xxxviii] And each US Senator represents an average of 3 million constituents.[xxxix] The likelihood of any of these individuals contacting their Representative or Senator is virtually nil. Adding one-hundred and seventy million people from Mexico and Canada will only make matters worse.

This is because there are only two ways such a "union" government can be arranged: The combined population of the three countries will be absorbed into the D.C. government, or an additional layer of government will be created on top of the D.C. government. Either way, the people lose.

If the population of Mexico and Canada are forced into the D.C. government, the US Congress would be tasked with representing over five-hundred million people. This would be a recipe for disaster. Not only would constituent-to-representative ratios skyrocket beyond current levels, but the sheer number of cultures, backgrounds, and viewpoints would be impossible to represent in one legislative body. The alternative would be to create an additional layer of government on top of what we already have in Washington. And just as the federal government is further removed from the people than the States, this additional layer of bureaucracy would be yet another step away from the people.

Sadly, both paths lead to the same result: the weakening and dilution of national legislatures, and the further distancing of the everyday citizen from his or her government. Unfortunately, this distancing leads to other, more dire consequences, like systemic corruption.

One example of this corruption is the US Congress. For several years, Senators and Representatives have achieved incredible profits from buying and selling stock. So much so that they enjoy a success rate that is twice as high as the most experienced Wall Street traders. Either members of the Senate and House just happen to be unparalleled geniuses when it comes to trading stocks, or they're using insider information to make themselves (and their friends) rich. Sadly, this kind of graft is business as usual in Washington, D.C.

The American people understand the Senate and House are essentially untouchable when it comes to investigations of corruption. Primarily because the only entity that can change Congress' behavior is Congress itself. And very few, if any, Congressmen are willing to put a stop to their money-making machine. With this kind of wickedness getting a free hand at the national level, one can only imagine the kind of opportunities for corruption that will present themselves in a supra-national body.

It's for these reasons (and many more) that we reject the importation of artificial governments that create more distance between themselves and the people. Fortunately, we're going in a different direction. The era of top-down, unaccountable governance is over. The peoples of the United States deserve a government that is adaptive to their needs and representative of their interests. And that's exactly what we'll get, when we build a new way.

How will the Military Work?

The North American military will function in much the same way as the United States military. Its primary responsibility will be the security and well-being of the North American Republic. The military will feature a professional, all-volunteer force of officers and enlisted men/women. And it maintains the principle of civilian control.

In North America, the military will be viewed for what it is: A lethal force that is designed to protect our Constitution and homeland. Not a testing ground for social experimentation. The NAR military will always strive to be the very best in the world. And it will train and equip each member of the Armed Forces to achieve their full potential.

Will We Still Have Our Constitutional Rights?

Yes. The United States Constitution remains the Supreme Law of the Land. All individual rights in the US Constitution are in effect in the North American Republic. The only modifications to the Constitution are to accommodate the structural changes of the Continental Government.

Will Other States/Provinces Be Allowed to Join the North American Republic?

Yes. If a foreign State/Province wishes to join the North American Republic, there are three steps it must take. First, it must hold a referendum in which a majority of its residents express their desire to join the NAR. Second, its State/Provincial legislature must vote in favor of same. Third, its State/Provincial Executive must agree with the legislature and sign off on the application.

After these steps have been completed, the North American legislature will study the issue and make a recommendation to accept or deny the new State/Province. If the NAR legislature is favorable to the request to join, three additional steps must be taken.

First, each of the Regional Republics will hold a referendum asking their citizens to vote on the issue. Foreign States/Provinces can only be approved by unanimous consent of the Regional Republics. If the majority of citizens of each of the six Republics vote in favor of accepting a foreign State/Province, the issue then goes before the North American legislature.

Second, the NAR legislature must vote on whether to accept the new State/Province into the North American Republic. This will require a majority vote from the House, and a 2/3 majority from the Senate. If the Continental Congress approves the acceptance of a new State/Province into the NAR, the issue then moves to the President of the North American Republic.

Third, the President of the North American Republic will either agree with the Continental legislature's recommendation or disagree. If the President agrees, then the State/Province in question is accepted into the North American Republic. If the

President disagrees, a 2/3 majority of Congress may override the President's objection. If this occurs, the new State/Province is accepted into the NAR.

It's important to note that no foreign State/Province may join one of the already-established six Regional Republics. A newly accepted State/Province will constitute a new Regional Republic. If multiple States/Provinces are accepted into the NAR, they will be combined into a geographically cohesive new Regional Republic.

When a new State/Province is accepted into the North American Republic, they must accept the US Constitution as the Supreme Law of the Land, have their citizens vote to approve a Constitution for their State and Regional Republic, and uphold all the other requirements of States and Regions of the NAR. There are no provinces in the North American Republic. So, an area that was previously known as a Province will be known as a State in the NAR.

Will the North American Republic still use the Electoral College?

Yes. The Founders were quite clear that the United States was never intended to be a direct democracy. As such, the North American Republic will continue to utilize the State-based Electoral College system for NAR Presidential Elections.

Will we need passports to travel from one Regional Republic to another?

No. The North American Republic features free trade and free travel among the States and Regional Republics. A valid State identification is all that is needed to drive, fly, or travel by train anywhere in the NAR. It's important to note, however, that each State and Regional Republic maintains their own laws and approaches to social issues.

If I want to visit foreign countries, what kind of passport will I need?

A North American Republic passport. International travel will operate much the same way it does today. Citizens who wish to travel to foreign countries must first acquire a North American Republic passport. Once this occurs, citizens are free to travel abroad.

How will the border work in the North American Republic?

The ultimate responsibility for international borders of the North American Republic rests with the Continental government. States and Regional Republics may supplement NAR forces at international borders. States and Regions are responsible for their own internal border security. The NAR operates under a free-travel and free-trade system. This means that a citizen of North America may travel freely throughout all the States and Regional Republics will no passports required.

Illegal immigration is not tolerated under NAR law. Neither the North American President, or any other member of the Executive Branch, has the authority to break laws concerning immigration or any other matter. Those who enter the NAR illegally will be detained, identified, questioned, provided emergency medical care as needed, and deported back to the country from which they originally crossed into the NAR.

What kind of money will we use?

The North American Dollar. The Dollar will be issued directly from the Continental Government. It will be legal tender for all debts, public and private. And it will be the official currency of all States and Regional Republics of the NAR. A digital dollar will be available, but the North American government will also issue cash. Additionally, the majority of retail stores will be required to accept cash as a form of payment for a period of at least fifty years after the founding of the Republic.

Will there be an official language of the North American Republic?

Yes. English is the official language of the North American Republic. Due to the incredible diversity of the Republic, having a common language that we all can communicate with is a necessity. This means that all business involving the North American government (both internally and in relations with States and Regional Republics) will be conducted in English.

Is space exploration a priority for the Continental Government?

Absolutely. In addition to the NAR Space Force, the Continental Government will work tirelessly with public and private entities to advance space exploration.

Will the North American Republic be a free-trade zone?

Yes. People and goods may move freely across the North American Republic. There are no internal passports required inside the NAR.

How will citizenship work?

A citizen will be both a citizen of the North American Republic as well as their Regional Republic. North American citizenship will be utilized most frequently when voting in Continental elections or traveling overseas. Regional citizenship will be utilized when voting in Regional elections. Citizens can only maintain citizenship in one Regional Republic at a time.

What's the NAR's attitude towards foreign nations?

North America desires peace and prosperity amongst all nations. The Republic will seek mutually beneficial "win-win" outcomes in all negotiations. North America will attempt to settle any disputes with negotiations first, while also utilizing modernized international structures to ensure peaceful resolutions.

Will the North American Republic keep the semi-annual time changes via the federal government?

No. Currently the United States features two time changes per year. In March, the people are instructed to set their clocks ahead one hour ("spring forward") to align with Daylight Savings Time. Then, in November, citizens are told to set their clocks back one hour ("fall back") to align with Standard Time. In theory, these semi-annual time changes are supposed to maximize energy efficiency by taking advantage of long summer nights. But the evidence supporting the usefulness of this idea is mixed at best.

This is because any energy savings accomplished by the DST system is counterbalanced by increases in negative health events like heart attacks, botched medical decisions, car accidents, etc. Hurting the citizenry to obtain a negligible increase in fuel efficiency makes little sense. As such, the NAR government will repeal the Uniform Time Act, and set all time zones in the United States to Standard Time.

What are the term limits for members of the North American Congress?

An individual may serve no more than two terms in the Senate, and three terms in the House of Representatives. These limits apply for the life of the individual.

Will dual citizens be allowed to hold elected office in the North American Republic?

No. A dual citizen, as currently defined, is a person who holds citizenship from both the United States as well as one or more foreign countries. The North American Republic prohibits dual citizens from obtaining any elected office in the Continental Government. Members of Congress are expected to represent the peoples of their districts, States, and Regions…not the interests of foreign governments.

How will North America help members of Generation Z?

Numerous ways. First, the NAR government will make substantial investments in Continental infrastructure. This will include Interstate Highways, seaports, bridges, dams, etc. Members of Gen Z (as well as everyone else) will be eligible to work on these projects. For each year completed in the Continental Infrastructure Program, workers will receive funding for one year of college, technical learning, or trade school, up to a total of four years.

Second, the NAR government will extend tax breaks for first-time home and automobile purchases. Buying a car and a house is a big part of the American Dream. It's important that members of Gen Z get to experience that.

Third, the Continental Government will ban usury throughout the North American Republic. This means that interest rates for things like credit cards, home and auto loans, etc., will be capped at five percent. This will help members of Generation Z, as well as everyone else, live a more fruitful and enjoyable life, free from the shackles of usury and debt.

Finally, the design of the North American Republic itself will be of great benefit to Zoomers. As each State and Republic features their own approach to life, people of all ages will be able to find a location that resonates with their beliefs. This will provide citizens of North America, especially Generation Z, with unlimited possibilities for the future.

9 FINAL THOUGHTS

The North American Republic is an idea whose time has come. It represents a natural and logical evolution of the ideals of our Founders. And it propels the American system well into the 21st century. Namely, by bringing government closer to home, and respecting the cultural differences of the peoples of North America.

Our current system is coming to an end. It has destroyed itself by over-centralization of power, reckless spending, endless wars, and ignoring the principles upon which America was founded. As many have come to realize, there is no fixing what is broken. Instead, we must find a new way. And that new way is the North American Republic.

When the Founding Fathers were designing the American system of governance, they decided upon the motto, "E Pluribus Unum" to represent their ultimate desire. Translated to English, the phrase means, "Out of Many, One". Throughout our 250 years of independence, various methods have been attempted to achieve this goal. From a loose confederation to a heavily-centralized empire. Yet none of them have ever truly succeeded.

Now, for the first time, we have a system that will accomplish the goal of uniting the peoples of America…and establishing liberty throughout the land. The North American Republic is that system.

The NAR harnesses the power of the diversity of America. It does so by recognizing the ideal time and place for divergence and unity. It's this flexibility that is the true strength of North America. And that strength is what unites us towards the common goals of peace and prosperity. Through the North American

Republic, we have found a new way. And through that new way, we will achieve the aspiration of our Founding Fathers: an America United, enjoying the fruits of liberty, at peace with itself and the world.

Out of Many, One.

--Kevin Newsom

10 ABOUT THE AUTHOR

Kevin Newsom is an American, born and raised in Texas. With ten years of experience in government, Kevin has first-hand knowledge of what works (and what doesn't) in the public sector. Like so many of his countrymen, Newsom is concerned with the rapid decline of the United States government. It's this concern that inspired him to write The New Way.

Kevin earned a Bachelor of Psychology from the University of Texas at Austin, and a Master of Public Administration from the University of Houston. He enjoys reading, studying history, watching college football, creating music, and spending time with friends and family.

You can view all of Kevin's works at: KevinNewsom.com

ENDNOTES

[i] Source: https://www.bea.gov/data/gdp/gdp-state

The GDP figures for North America and its Republics are based on 2022 data via the BEA website. It is a reasonable estimation of current GDP. These figures also take into consideration various counties that have moved from one Regional Republic to another.

The writer generally prefers the use of Purchasing Power Parity (PPP) to describe economic rankings. Unfortunately, that kind of data was not as readily available (or reliable) as the GDP information. Much like real life, artists must make use of the tools they have at their disposal.

Additional Source for Land Mass: https://worldpopulationreview.com/state-rankings/states-by-area

[ii]

Sources: https://www.census.gov/quickfacts/AK & https://www.usaspending.gov/state/alaska/latest

https://alaskabeacon.com/2022/11/03/angst-over-youth-outmigration-emerges-in-alaska-campaign-rhetoric-and-debates/

[iii] https://www2.ed.gov/about/landing.jhtml

[iv] https://www.usaspending.gov/agency/department-of-education?fy=2023

[v] https://www.thedefensepost.com/2023/12/15/us-2024-defense-budget/

[vi]

https://responsiblestatecraft.org/2023/01/04/failing-f-35-grounded-once-again/

[vii] https://www.transportation.gov/sites/dot.gov/files/2023-03/BudgetHL2024_Mar09_3pm_508.pdf

[viii]

https://www.hhs.gov/sites/default/files/fy-2023-budget-in-brief.pdf

[ix]

https://www.reuters.com/legal/government/paramount-importance-judge-orders-fda-hasten-release-pfizer-vaccine-docs-2022-01-07/

[x]

https://www.hud.gov/about/mission

[xi] https://nlihc.org/sites/default/files/CHCDF_Webinar_FY23-24_021023.pdf

[xii]   https://thecradle.co/articles/the-historic-us-saudi-relationship-cannot-bounce-back

[xiii]   https://www.gonewsindia.com/latest-news/international/saudi-arabia-to-trade-oil-in-yuan-how-will-it-affect-india-28542

[xiv]   https://www.dhs.gov/sites/default/files/2023-03/DHS%20FY%202024%20BUDGET%20IN%20BRIEF%20%28BIB%29_Remediated.pdf

[xv]   https://www.uscourts.gov/statistics-reports/federal-judicial-caseload-statistics-2021

[xvi] https://www.crfb.org/blogs/saving-us-postal-service

[xvii] https://www.amtrak.com/about-amtrak.html

[xviii]   https://www.ers.usda.gov/webdocs/outlooks/105762/bio-05.pdf?v=5239.1

[xix] https://www.statista.com/statistics/686193/production-of-corn-us/

[xx] https://www.spglobal.com/commodityinsights/en/market-insights/latest-news/lng/111323-north-americas-lng-export-capacity-expected-to-double-by-2027-eia

[xxi]   https://www.gao.gov/blog/american-credit-card-debt-hits-new-record-whats-changed-post-pandemic

[xxii]   https://www.americanbar.org/groups/crsj/publications/human_rights_magazine_home/wealth-disparities-in-civil-rights/federal-policies-trap-tribes-in-poverty/

[xxiii]   https://www.reuters.com/world/asia-pacific/japan-set-release-fukushima-water-amid-criticism-seafood-import-bans-2023-08-23/

[xxiv]   https://www.cnn.com/2022/09/08/us/jackson-flint-water-crisis-trust/index.html

[xxv]   https://www.cnbc.com/2022/10/13/what-is-solar-geoengineering-sunlight-reflection-risks-and-benefits.html

[xxvi]   https://communitygreening.org/blog/six-benefits-of-urban-forestry-trees

[xxvii]   https://www.peta.org/blog/contracted-beagle-breeding-factory-other-nih-atrocities/

[xxviii]   https://www.mentalhealth.va.gov/docs/data-sheets/2023/2023-National-Veteran-Suicide-Prevention-Annual-Report-FINAL-508.pdf

[xxix]   https://www.census.gov/newsroom/stories/poverty-awareness-month.html

[xxx]   https://www.feedingamerica.org/take-action/advocate/effects-of-federal-budget-on-hunger

[xxxi]   https://www.pgpf.org/blog/2024/02/what-is-the-national-debt-costing-us

[xxxii]   https://www.cato.org/commentary/750-bases-80-countries-too-many-any-nation-time-us-bring-its-troops-home

[xxxiii]   https://www.defense.gov/casualty.pdf

[xxxiv]   https://www.washingtonpost.com/world/2023/05/15/war-on-ter-

ror-911-deaths-afghanistan-iraq/

[xxxv] Ibid.

[xxxvi] https://www.un.org/en/our-work/maintain-international-peace-and-security

[xxxvii] https://www.moneygeek.com/living/states-most-reliant-federal-government/

[xxxviii] https://www2.census.gov/programs-surveys/decennial/2020/data/apportionment/apportionment-2020-tableC2.pdf
[xxxix]

https://www.thegreenpapers.com/Census10/FedRep.phtml